# Still Nut...
# CHOCOLATE

We think Norman may
enjoy some of these
recipes!!
Happy memories of our
holiday in Canada

June 1998
Shirley & Ray

Purchased at Elaine's
in Lillovet

*Susan Mendelson & Deborah Roitberg*

Douglas & McIntyre
Vancouver/Toronto

*Dedicated to the loving memory of Sylvie*

Douglas & McIntyre
1615 Venables Street
Vancouver, British Columbia
V5L 2H1

**Canadian Cataloguing in Publication Data**

Mendelson, Susan, 1952–
  Still nuts about chocolate


   ISBN 0-55054-056-4


  1.  Cookery (Chocolate)   2.  Desserts.   I.  Roitberg, Deborah, 1951–
II.  Title.   III.  Title: Nuts about chocolate.
TX767.C5M46 1992        641.6'374        C92-091464-0

Editing by Barbara Pulling
Design by Rose Cowles
Photography by Derek Murray
Photo credits: Stone tiles on front cover courtesy Ann Sacks Tile & Stone.
Thanks to Eaton's, Georg Jensen, Industrial Revolution, Inform, Kaya Kaya,
Tile Town and W. H. Puddifoot.
Typeset by The Typeworks
Printed and bound in Canada by D. W. Friesen & Sons Ltd.

# CONTENTS

# INTRODUCTION

It's hard to believe that it's just nine years since *Nuts about Chocolate* was first published. We've received laudatory letters from many of you, and we are constantly delighted to hear that restaurants and hotels are using our recipes. *Chocolatier* magazine published our Pecan Glazed Torte recipe, and an international ice-cream company has even named one of their flavours after our book.

Chocolate continues to be the universal favourite food, and today the finest chocolates in the world are available in most markets, enabling us to enjoy even more of the best. But trends have changed, new ideas are upon us and we have had requests from all across the country for more of our creations. So here are 60 delicious new recipes, as well as new versions of some of your old favourites. We think you'll be as delighted as we are with these new desserts. And your family and guests will never know how easy they are to make— unless you tell them!

In our opinion, a cookbook is worth the price of purchase if it introduces you to one or two fabulous recipes that you can make time and time again. We hope you'll find a couple of new treats here to add to your repertoire. That way, *Still Nuts about Chocolate* will be the best kind of bargain—the kind you really need!

Susan and Deborah

# Acknowledgements

Thanks to Jack Amar, Jack Lutsky, Mother Roz, Mother Jeanette, Grandma Selma, Grandma Faye, Lynn Mendelson, Sandi Amorim, Roberta Braidner, Belinda D'Souza, Anna de Flores, Barbie Glynn, Linda Gold, Barbara Halparin, Frederique Leroy, Greta Levy, Lana Lipkowitz, Miriam Lutsky, Neiman-Marcus, Martha Miller, Carol Roitberg, Carol Slater and Jeannie Watchuk.

# WORKING WITH CHOCOLATE

There are three things to keep in mind when working with chocolate:
1 Chocolate burns easily.
2 Water, even a drop, added to chocolate can cause problems.
3 Chocolate may not be chocolate.

Here are our recommendations:

When melting chocolate, chop it into uniform bits; place in the top of a *clean, completely dry* double boiler over HOT not BOILING water. NEVER COVER. Always melt chocolate slowly over low heat. (Think of it as you would frozen butter—if a large chunk is placed over direct heat it will fry and burn, but it will melt without burning if you cut it into small bits and melt it over low heat.) When the chocolate is almost melted, remove from the heat and stir until just melted.

If you are melting chocolate in a microwave oven, use medium heat for semi-sweet chocolate and low heat for white and milk chocolate. Do not cover. Chocolate will hold its shape even when melted, so you'll need to stir it with a spoon (or dip your finger in!) every 20 seconds to check. Melted chocolate should be warm, not hot, for baking.

If a drop or two of moisture should land on the chocolate, it can cause the chocolate to "tighten" or "seize." Don't panic. Stir in about a teaspoon (*5 mL*) of vegetable oil or shortening per ounce (*30 g*) of chocolate, and all will be saved.

Always read labels when buying chocolate to make sure you are getting the real thing. Pure chocolate has been made with either chocolate liqueur or cocoa butter. Anything else is a "chocolate flavoured" synthetic.

# PLAYING WITH CHOCOLATE

## Chocolate Curls

To make these decorations, melt semi-sweet chocolate together with a tsp. (*5 mL*) of oil for each 2 oz. (*60 g*) of chocolate and pour onto a flat surface. (We prefer a cold marble slab, but any flat surface will do.) Spread the chocolate so that it is even and very thin. When it starts to lose its shine and is firm but not hard, it's time to start the curls. Holding a metal spatula (a pancake flipper works well) at a 45° angle, push against the chocolate until it forms a large curl. (The motion is a little like shovelling snow.) Let the curls dry until firm, then store in an airtight container in a cool place. Use the spatula to lift the curls into the container; fingerprints will leave marks on the chocolate.

Smaller curls can be made using a vegetable peeler against a block of chocolate (at room temperature); this works especially well with the softer chocolates such as European fondants. To avoid marking the chocolate, hold the block with waxed paper.

## Chocolate Flowers

Cut three sheets of waxed paper, 6" × 1½" (*15 cm × 4 cm*). Melt the chocolate and paint it onto the paper using a pastry brush. Refrigerate until firm but not hard — about 5 minutes. Carefully peel the chocolate off the paper, curling it around itself as tightly as possible. Continue until you have a flower of the desired size. If it is not exactly to your liking, throw the chocolate back into the pot and start again.

## Chocolate Leaves

Flat, waxy leaves like those from camellia bushes make the best moulds. Clean and dry them well. Melt semi-sweet chocolate and, using a pastry brush, paint the chocolate on the *underside* of the leaf, coating evenly. Wipe away any excess chocolate from the front or sides of the leaf. Place on a sheet of waxed paper, uncoated side down, in the refrigerator for 8–10 minutes, until chocolate is hardened. Beginning at the stem end, carefully peel away the leaf. Voila! A magnificent chocolate leaf. For a professional look, handle as little as possible.

CAUTION: Be sure the leaf you use is nontoxic.

# INGREDIENTS &
# PREPARATION

In our recipes we use all-purpose flour, light vegetable oil (our preference is for cold-pressed sunflower oil), white granulated sugar (unless otherwise specified), fresh lemon juice (although bottled juice can be substituted if absolutely necessary), and pure vanilla extract. We always use pure, unsweetened cocoa powder. We generally prefer Dutch processed (alkalized) cocoa since it has a richer colour and is less acidic than the natural (nonalkalized) variety. Either can be used in these recipes, however. Liquid and solid honey are interchangeable—we usually use liquid—and when brown sugar is called for it can be either light or dark. All brown sugar measurements call for sugar to be loosely packed. Butter can be salted or unsalted, but we prefer unsalted since it lets the other flavours come through. When a recipe requires the butter to be creamed, it should be brought to room temperature first.

Eggs should always be room temperature before using. Because of the danger of salmonella bacteria, we have adapted most recipes that call for raw eggs. The addition of a sugar syrup that has been cooked to 240°F (*115°C*) raises the temperature sufficiently to assure safety.

Bitter chocolate is unsweetened; bittersweet chocolate is semi-sweet. To cut chocolate that has hardened, first score the surface with a very sharp knife, then cut through it. This method will prevent cracking.

Always toast nuts before chopping them, but watch that they do not burn. Spread the nuts on a cookie sheet, place in a 350°F (*180°C*) oven and toast as follows:

|  |  |
|---|---|
| Walnuts | 7–8 minutes |
| Pecans | 7–8 minutes |
| Peanuts | 12–15 minutes |
| Hazelnuts | 14–15 minutes |
| Almonds | 16–18 minutes |

Flaked nuts take less toasting time than whole ones.

To prepare pans, either smear with butter and dust flour over the surface until the butter is well-coated *or* line the pan with waxed paper or parchment paper cut to the size of its bottom.

# CHOCOLATE

## Cointreau Fudge Cake

Preheat oven to 350°F (*180°C*)

| | |
|---|---|
| 1½ cups (*375 mL*) soft butter<br>6 oz. (*170 g*) soft cream cheese<br>3 cups (*750 mL*) light brown sugar | Using electric mixer, cream butter and cream cheese. Gradually add sugar until mixture is light and fluffy. |
| 5 eggs | Add eggs one at a time, mixing after each addition. |
| 4 oz. (*115 g*) unsweetened chocolate, melted and slightly cooled | Add. |
| 1 cup (*250 mL*) buttermilk or yogurt | Add all at once. (The mixture will look as if it's curdling, but not to worry.) |
| 3 cups (*750 mL*) flour<br>2½Tbsp. (*40 mL*) orange rind, finely grated | Gradually add and blend well. |

1 cup (*250 mL*) boiling water
2 tsp. (*10 mL*) baking soda
2 Tbsp. (*30 mL*) Cointreau
liqueur
} Combine and fold into batter.

Pour into three prepared, round 9″ (*23 cm*) cake pans. Bake for 25–30 minutes until toothpick comes out clean. Let sit for 30 minutes in pans before removing. Ice and chill.

# Cointreau Icing

½ cup (*125 mL*) soft butter — Cream until smooth.

1 cup (*250 mL*) soft cream cheese — Add and beat well.

4 oz. (*115 g*) unsweetened chocolate, melted and slightly cooled — Add.

4 cups (*1 L*) icing sugar — Add.

2 Tbsp. (*30 mL*) Cointreau
2 Tbsp. (*30 mL*) orange juice concentrate
Rind of one orange, finely grated
} Add and beat until fluffy.

This amount will fill and frost top and sides of a three-layer cake.

*Chocolate and orange are wonderfully complementary flavours and when added to both cake and icing, the result is irresistible.*

# Double Fudge Chocolate Cake

Preheat oven to 350°F *(180°C)*

| | |
|---|---|
| 2 eggs<br>1 cup *(250 mL)* sugar<br>2 Tbsp. *(30 mL)* soft butter<br>1 cup *(250 mL)* oil<br>½ cup *(125 mL)* cocoa, packed<br>½ cup *(125 mL)* buttermilk<br>1 tsp. *(5 mL)* vanilla | Beat in this order, adding ingredients one at a time. |
| 2¼ cups *(550 mL)* flour<br>1½ tsp. *(7 mL)* baking soda<br>1½ tsp *(7 mL)* baking powder | Sift together and add to above mixture. |
| 1 cup *(250 mL)* boiling water | Fold in. |
| ½ cup *(125 mL)* chocolate chips | |

Place mixture in two prepared, round 8″ or 9″ *(20–23 cm)* cake pans. Sprinkle with chocolate chips. Bake for 25 minutes. Ice with our Incredible Chocolate Icing.

*For years, this was our guarded secret. Our customers call it the Definitive Chocolate Cake. As a double bonus, you now get our Incredible Chocolate Icing recipe.*

# Incredible Chocolate Icing

| | |
|---|---|
| ½ cup *(125 mL)* soft butter<br>1 cup *(250 mL)* icing sugar<br>⅔ cup *(150 mL)* cocoa | Place in food processor and, using steel knife, blend for 4 seconds. |
| 1 tsp. *(5 mL)* vanilla<br>2 Tbsp. *(30 mL)* milk<br>2 Tbsp. *(30 mL)* hot coffee | Add liquid and blend until smooth. Additional milk will make a thinner icing. |

You can combine these ingredients with an electric mixer, but the texture will not be as smooth.

# Coco Glaäze or the Best Chocolate Ice Cream

| | |
|---|---|
| 3½ oz. (*100 g*) bittersweet chocolate | Melt and set aside. |
| 4 egg yolks | Beat until light in colour. |
| ⅔ cup (*150 mL*) sugar | Gradually add to yolks. Beat well until creamy and pale. |
| 2 cups (*500 mL*) whole milk | Bring to a boil. Slowly add a bit of boiling milk to yolk mixture. Then add yolk mixture back into rest of milk, whisking to avoid curdling. Pour melted chocolate into mixture. |
| ¼ cup (*50 mL*) unsweetened cocoa | Add to chocolate mixture. Cook over medium heat until thick enough to coat spoon (approximately 150°F/*65°C*). Stir constantly. Do not boil. Set aside. |
| 2 Tbsp. (*30 mL*) sugar }<br>2 tsp. (*10 mL*) water } | Combine and cook to deep golden caramel without stirring. Add to custard and blend. |
| | Cool in fridge for at least ½ hour, until cold. Transfer to ice cream maker. |

Optional:

| | |
|---|---|
| ½ cup (*125 mL*) hazelnuts, coarsely ground | Add if desired while ice cream is in maker. |

*It really is the best! Try a blindfold test with any other European-style ice cream.*

# White Chocolate Ginger Truffles

| | |
|---|---|
| ¼ cup (*75 mL*) heavy cream | Bring to boil in small saucepan. |
| 6 oz. (*170 g*) white chocolate, finely chopped | Add to cream and stir to melt. |
| 2 Tbsp. (*30 mL*) candied ginger, finely chopped<br>1 Tbsp. (*15 mL*) preserved ginger, finely chopped<br>1 Tbsp. (*15 mL*) preserved ginger syrup | Add to mixture. Pour into bowl and freeze until firm (about 30 minutes). |

Line baking sheet with waxed paper and dust with icing sugar. Spoon 16 mounds (about 1 Tbsp./*15 mL* each) onto sheet and roll into balls. Freeze until firm (30 minutes minimum) or up to 1 month.

### Before Serving:

| | |
|---|---|
| 6 oz. (*180 g*) white chocolate, melted | Dip frozen truffles individually. Sprinkle with additional chopped ginger as desired. |
| | Serve cool or at room temperature. |

*Elegance itself.*

# New Unbelievable Chocolate Mousse

|  |  |
|---|---|
| ⅔ cup (*150 mL*) sugar<br>⅓ cup (*75 mL*) water | Stir over low heat until sugar is dissolved. Then boil for 1½ minutes. |
| 6 oz. (*170 g*) semi-sweet chocolate chunks<br>4 oz. (*115 g*) unsweetened chocolate | Melt together and set aside. |
| 5 egg yolks | Process in food processor, slowly adding ½ of the boiling syrup.<br><br>Keep processor running as you execute the following steps:<br><br>Add melted chocolate to syrup/yolk mixture. |
| 3 Tbsp. (*45 mL*) brandy | Add to above. |
| 4 Tbsp. (*60 mL*) soft butter | Add to above mixture a little at a time. Turn off processor.<br><br>Pour mixture into a bowl. |
| 5 egg whites | Beat whites until stiff. Gradually add the rest of the hot syrup, then fold into chocolate mixture.<br><br>Chill 3–4 hours before serving, or use in other recipes. |

## Variations

For Chocolate Orange Mousse use 3 Tbsp. (*45 mL*) orange-flavoured liqueur.
For Hazelnut Mousse use 3 Tbsp. (*45 mL*) Frangelico and top with crushed hazelnuts.
For Mocha Mousse use 3 Tbsp. (*45 mL*) coffee-flavoured liqueur.

*An easy chocolate mousse made with cooked, not raw, eggs.*

# Your Basic Chocolate Cheesecake

Preheat oven to 350°F *(180°C)*.

## Chocolate Crust

| | |
|---|---|
| 1⅓ cups ( *325 mL*) chocolate wafers, crushed<br>⅓ cup *(75 mL)* melted butter | Mix and press into a 9″ or 10″ *(23–25 cm)* springform pan. Bake for 5 minutes. |
| 1 lb. *(500 g)* soft cream cheese<br>⅔ cup *(150 mL)* sour cream<br>½ cup *(125 mL)* sugar<br>2 tsp. *(10 mL)* vanilla | Combine and beat until smooth. |
| 6 oz. *(170 g)* semi-sweet chocolate<br>1 oz. *(30 g)* bitter chocolate | Melt over hot water and add to mixture, beating until smooth. |
| 2 large eggs | Add and beat for 5 minutes. |

Pour mixture into crust. Bake 35–40 minutes. Let sit until cake reaches room temperature, then chill 2 hours.

## Variations

Omit vanilla and add in its place:

| | |
|---|---|
| 1 Tbsp. *(15 mL)* brandy | For Chocolate Brandy Cheesecake |
| 1 Tbsp. *(15 mL)* orange juice concentrate<br>1 Tbsp. *(15 mL)* orange liqueur | For Chocolate Orange Cheesecake |
| 1 Tbsp. *(15 mL)* almond liqueur<br>1 tsp. *(5 mL)* almond extract | For Chocolate Amaretto Cheesecake |

## Toppings

For Your Basic Chocolate Cheesecake:

| | |
|---|---|
| 1 cup *(250 mL)* heavy cream<br>2 Tbsp. *(30 mL)* icing sugar<br>1 tsp. *(5 mL)* vanilla | Beat until soft peaks form. Spread over chilled chocolate. Chill 1 hour before serving. |

# Recipes

For Sour Cream Topping:

1 cup (*250 mL*) sour cream
1 Tbsp. (*15 mL*) your favourite flavouring
2 Tbsp. (*30 mL*) sugar

} Mix and spoon gently over cheesecake and return to oven for 5 minutes.

Sprinkle with shaved chocolate and/or nuts. Chill 2–3 hours before serving.

*The combination of cheese and chocolate may at first sound peculiar, but this cheesecake will change your concept about life in general!*

# White Chocolate Ice Cream

1 cup (*250 mL*) milk
¼ cup (*50 mL*) sugar
1 cup (*250 mL*) heavy cream
4 egg yolks
Pinch of salt

} Combine and whisk over medium–low heat until thick enough to coat spoon.

4–5 oz. (*120–150 g*) white chocolate, finely chopped
1½ tsp. (*7 mL*) vanilla

} Add to above and stir until chocolate is melted. Cool to room temperature.

Refrigerate until cold (1 hour or more).

½ cup (*125 mL*) buttermilk
2 Tbsp. (*30 mL*) fresh lemon juice

} Stir into chocolate mixture and transfer to ice cream maker.

*The lemon juice adds a refreshing quality.*

# Chocolate

## Wonder Sauce

| | |
|---|---|
| 3 oz. (*90 g*) unsweetened chocolate<br>¼ cup (*50 mL*) butter<br>½ cup (*125 mL*) sugar<br>½ cup (*125 mL*) water | Combine and place in double boiler over hot, not boiling, water. Stirring occasionally, cook 5–10 minutes until smooth. |
| 1 tsp. (*5 mL*) vanilla | Stir in. |

Refrigerate to thicken. Makes about ¾ cup (*175 mL*).

*Made from ingredients everyone has on hand, this sauce is great when the urge for a hot fudge sundae suddenly strikes.*

## Almost Instant Hot Fudge Sauce

| | |
|---|---|
| ⅓ cup (*75 mL*) sugar<br>⅓ cup (*75 mL*) water | Combine in saucepan. Cook over medium heat to dissolve sugar, stirring constantly. Bring to boil for 2–3 minutes. Remove from heat. |
| 6 oz. (*170 g*) semi-sweet chocolate<br>2 oz. (*60 g*) unsweetened chocolate<br>¼ cup (*50 mL*) butter | Melt together in separate pan. Whisk syrup mixture into melted chocolate. |
| ½ cup (*125 mL*) evaporated milk | Whisk in. |
| 1–2 tsp. (*5–10 mL*) vanilla | Add. |

*What could be easier?*

# White Chocolate Mousse

| | |
|---|---|
| 12 oz. (*340 g*) white chocolate | Melt, then allow to cool until warm. |
| 3 cups (*750 mL*) heavy cream | Whip cream and set aside. (Cream should be stiff.) |
| 4 egg yolks<br>¾ cup (*175 mL*) sugar | In large bowl beat yolks until pale yellow, then add sugar gradually. |
| 2 pkgs. gelatine (2 Tbsp./*30 mL*)<br>¼ cup (*50 mL*) warm water } | Soften gelatine in water. Heat to dissolve if necessary. |
| | Add a small amount of egg yolk mixture to gelatine, then combine gelatine mixture with yolks and beat vigorously. |
| | Gradually add melted chocolate, using low speed on food processor or electric mixer. (If mixture is not completely smooth, reheat in double boiler to dissolve lumps.) Then gently add whipped cream. |

Chill until set. Serve topped with toasted almonds or fresh berries in season.

*This exotic version can be layered with our dark chocolate mousse for an interesting display of textures, but — each layer must be thoroughly chilled before adding the next.*

# Chocolate

## German Chocolate Cake

### Genoise

|  |  |
|---|---|
|  | Preheat oven to 350°F (*180°C*). |
| 6 eggs | Beat 8–10 minutes until very light and fluffy. |
| 1 cup (*250 mL*) sugar<br>1 tsp. (*5 mL*) vanilla | Add to eggs very gradually, beating on high. |
| ½ cup (*125 mL*) flour<br>½ cup (*125 mL*) cocoa | Sift a little at a time over eggs and fold in. |
| 10 Tbsp. (*150 mL*) butter, melted and slightly cooled | Add, 2 Tbsp. (*30 mL*) at a time, folding in gently. |

Prepare three round 8″ or 9″ (*20–23 cm*) cake pans. Gently pour mixture into the pans, dividing equally. Bake for 10–15 minutes.

### Filling

|  |  |
|---|---|
| 1 egg<br>½ cup (*125 mL*) sugar<br>1 Tbsp. (*15 mL*) flour<br>1 cup (*250 mL*) sour cream<br>½ cup (*125 mL*) raisins, coarsely chopped with<br>1 Tbsp. (*15 mL*) flour | Mix in top of double boiler and cook over medium heat until thick, stirring constantly. Let cool 15 minutes. |
| ½ cup (*125 mL*) threaded coconut, toasted<br>½ cup (*125 mL*) pecans, coarsely chopped<br>1 tsp. (*5 mL*) vanilla<br>1 tsp. (*5 mL*) lemon juice | Add to above. |
|  | Makes about 2½ cups (*625 mL*). |
| Incredible Chocolate Icing<br>(page 10) |  |

# Recipes

## To Assemble

Spread layers and top of Genoise with filling. Ice sides and, if you're feeling wicked, decorate with rosettes of icing.

# Sex by Chocolate

| | |
|---|---|
| 15 oz. (*425 g*) bittersweet chocolate<br>1 cup (*250 mL*) heavy cream<br>2 Tbsp. (*30 mL*) unsalted butter | Combine in top of double boiler over simmering water and cook for 10 minutes. |
| 4 egg yolks | Add yolks, whisking until blended. |
| 1 cup (*250 mL*) icing sugar, sifted | Gradually add, beating until mixture is shiny. |
| ½ cup (*125 mL*) Frangelico liqueur | Blend in. |
| | Line a 3–cup (*750-mL*) terrine mold or loaf pan with plastic wrap and fill with mixture. Refrigerate overnight. |
| | Invert and carefully unmold. Take chill off for about ½ hour before serving. |
| | Cover top and sides with Mirror Glaze (p. 27) if you wish. |

Because there are uncooked eggs in this recipe, it should be refrigerated between servings. Be sure to serve within 48 hours. Cut with a hot knife.

*An often-requested recipe from the Lazy Gourmet. Now* this *is safe sex!*

# Chocolate

## Mint Truffle Torte

Chocolate Genoise (page 18) — Make Genoise in three round 8" or 9" (20–23 cm) cake pans. With fork or toothpicks make holes in Genoise and pour mint syrup over.

### Mint Syrup

1 cup (250 mL) sugar
1 cup (250 mL) water
1½ oz. (45 g) bitter chocolate, grated — Bring to boil. Add to sugar mixture and stir until chocolate is melted.

1½ tsp. (7 mL) peppermint extract — Add.

When syrup reaches room temperature, pour over Genoise.

### Crème Ganache

2 cups (500 mL) heavy cream — Bring to boil; remove from heat.

12 oz. (350 g) semi-sweet chocolate, grated or 12 oz. (350 g) chocolate chips — Pour chocolate into cream and whisk vigorously until well blended.

½ cup (125 mL) Crème de Menthe — Add liqueur.

Chill. When cold, whip until smooth and thick.

### To Assemble

Start with a layer of syrup-filled cake. Spread with ganache. Add another layer of cake, then another layer of ganache. End with a layer of cake. Ice top and sides with ganache and decorate with rosettes of ganache or green mints.

*This torte is better after sitting for a day or two, but you'll have to hide it or risk being the victim of the great chocolate disappearing act.*

# Chocolate Decadence Torte

Preheat oven to 425°F (*220°C*).

| | |
|---|---|
| 1 lb. (*500 g*) semi-sweet chocolate<br>¾ cup (*175 mL*) butter | Melt together in double boiler, then pour into bowl and set aside. |
| 4 eggs<br>2 tsp. (*10 mL*) sugar | In clean double boiler, combine and place over hot water; heat until warm. Then beat on high speed until cool and quadrupled in volume (about 8–10 minutes). |
| 1 Tbsp. (*15 mL*) flour | Sift over egg mixture and fold in. |
| 2 tsp. (*10 mL*) vanilla | Fold in. |
| | Gently fold one-third egg mixture into chocolate mixture, then fold in remaining eggs. |

Carefully pour into prepared 8″ or 9″ (*20–23 cm*) springform pan. Bake for 15 minutes. (It will sink a bit in the centre. DON'T WORRY!) Let cool and then freeze immediately.

## To Decorate

| | |
|---|---|
| 1 cup (*250 mL*) heavy cream<br>1 Tbsp. (*15 mL*) icing sugar | Whip to soft peaks. |

Place sweetened cream in pastry bag with star tip and play! Serve chilled.

*This recipe has swept North America as the indulgent dessert. We sometimes serve it with raspberry sauce (page 63) to cut the richness.*

# Chocolate

## Triple Chocolate Terrine

Line a 6-cup (*1.5-L*) terrine or loaf pan with waxed paper to overlap all sides by 2″ (*5 cm*). Smooth out wrinkles as much as possible.

### Yolk Mixture

| | |
|---|---|
| 1½ tsp. (*7 mL*) gelatin<br>½ cup (*125 mL*) milk | Combine in top of double boiler. Let soften 5 minutes, then place the pan directly over heat and bring to a boil, stirring constantly. Remove from heat. |
| 1 tsp. (*5 mL*) vanilla | Add. |
| 8 egg yolks | Whisk together, then slowly add ½ of milk mixture. Add yolk mixture back into rest of milk. Set over simmering, *not* boiling, water. Heat and whisk until candy thermometer reads 160°F (*71°C*). Mixture may appear curdled. Don't worry! Strain through fine sieve into measuring cup. |

### Step 1

| | |
|---|---|
| ⅓ yolk mixture<br>6 oz. (*170 g*) semi-sweet chocolate, melted | Beat 1 minute on high speed until smooth. |
| ⅞ cup (*200 mL*) heavy cream | Whip to firm peaks, then whisk a large dollop into chocolate mixture. Gently fold in the rest. |
| | Turn into lined pan. Rap sharply on counter to even out, then cover and freeze for 20–30 minutes (or until firm enough to support next layer). |

## Step 2

½ tsp. *(2 mL)* gelatin
1½ Tbsp. *(25 mL)* cognac } Combine in small cup or bowl and let soften for 5 minutes. Then heat in pan over medium heat until smooth or microwave. Remove from heat.

⅓ yolk mixture

Beat with cognac mixture until smooth.

6 oz. *(170 g)* white chocolate, melted

Gradually add to above. Beat until smooth.

⅞ cup *(200 mL)* heavy cream

Whip to stiff peaks. Whisk in several dollops to lighten texture of white chocolate mixture, then gently fold in the rest. Spread on top of dark chocolate layer, cover and freeze for 20–30 minutes.

## Step 3

⅓ yolk mixture
¾ tsp. *(3 mL)* instant espresso powder } Beat together until smooth and coffee is dissolved.

6 oz. *(170 g)* milk chocolate, melted

Beat with espresso mixture until smooth.

⅞ cup *(200 mL)* heavy cream

Whip to stiff peaks and add in two steps, as above.

Spread on top of white chocolate layer. Smooth. Refrigerate at least 4 hours.

Remove from refrigerator. Dip pan in hot water for 5 seconds, then unmold onto platter. Serve with Crème Anglaise (p. 63).

*This dessert manages to be both very rich and very light.*

## Chocolate Cherry Dome Pie

8 oz. *(250 g)* pitted cherries
(Use fresh when in season)
3 Tbsp. *(45 mL)* kirsch } Soak ahead at least 1 hour.

Prepare 10" *(25 cm)* pie shell (either chocolate or plain pastry) and bake at 350°F *(180°C)* for 20 minutes.

1 cup *(250 mL)* soft butter
¾ cup *(175 mL)* icing sugar } Combine in bowl and beat with electric mixer on high speed until fluffy.

½ cup *(125 mL)* cocoa — Sift in cocoa and blend.

8 oz. *(250 g)* semi-sweet chocolate, melted and slightly cooled — Add slowly to cocoa mixture, beating in.

1 egg — Beat in.

1 cup *(250 mL)* heavy cream — Add and beat until very fluffy — at least 5 minutes.

Add kirsch in which cherries were soaked.

Pour three-quarters of mixture into pastry shell. Press cherries into surface. Cover with rest of chocolate mixture, creating a dome effect.

4 oz. *(115 g)* semi-sweet chocolate
½ tsp. *(2 mL)* butter } Melt in double boiler. Let cool and gently pour over pie.

With a sharp knife score sections to be cut (about 14). Chill.

*Even lighter than our mousse!*

# Chocolate Heaven Pie

| | |
|---|---|
| 9″ or 10″ (*23–25 cm*) Chocolate Crust (page 33) | Prebake at 400°F (*200°C*) for 10 minutes. |
| 2 egg whites<br>1½ tsp. (*7 mL*) vinegar<br>½ tsp. (*2 mL*) salt<br>1 tsp. (*5 mL*) cinnamon | Combine and beat until soft peaks form. |
| ½ cup (*125 mL*) sugar | Gradually add sugar until stiff peaks form. |
| | Spread over pie shell and bake at 325°F (*160°C*) for 15–18 minutes until brown. Cool. |
| ⅓ cup (*75 mL*) Bittersweet Fudge Sauce (page 35) | Drizzle with sauce. |
| 1 cup (*250 mL*) heavy cream | Beat cream. |
| ⅓ cup (*75 mL*) chocolate chips, melted and slightly cooled<br>1 egg yolk<br>1 Tbsp. (*15 mL*) milk | Add chocolate, yolk and milk and beat until thick. Spread over sauce. |
| 1 cup (*250 mL*) heavy cream<br>½ tsp. (*2 mL*) cinnamon<br>¼ cup (*50 mL*) icing sugar | Beat until soft peaks form. Spread over chocolate, or pipe using pastry bag with large tip for a professional look. |
| ½ cup (*125 mL*) chocolate chips | Decorate with chocolate curls (page 5). |
| | Chill. |

*Heaven on earth!*

# Cassata

### Filling

3 cups *(750 mL)* ricotta cheese
¾ cup *(175 mL)* sugar } Blend together.

1½ Tbsp. *(25 mL)* grated orange peel
4 oz. *(115 g)* semi-sweet chocolate, finely chopped

Add and blend.

Set aside and chill.

Preheat oven to 350°F *(180°C)*.

### Italian Sponge Cake

4 egg whites — Beat until soft peaks form.

¼ cup *(50 mL)* sugar — Gradually add sugar and beat until stiff peaks form.

4 egg yolks — In separate bowl beat yolks until light.

⅓ cup *(75 mL)* sugar — Gradually add sugar to yolks and beat.
Gently fold whites into yolks.

¾ cup *(175 mL)* flour
1 tsp. *(5 mL)* baking powder } Sift over egg mixture and gently fold in.

Pour into prepared loaf pan and bake for 35 minutes. Invert on rack to cool.

### Syrup

⅓ cup *(75 mL)* sugar
⅓ cup *(75 mL)* water } Combine in saucepan over medium heat and let boil for 30 seconds. Remove from heat and cool for 5 minutes.

# Recipes

| | |
|---|---|
| 2 Tbsp. *(30 mL)* Cointreau or orange liqueur<br>2 Tbsp. *(30 mL)* brandy | Add to cooled mixture. |

Incredible Chocolate Icing
(page 10)

## To Assemble

Slice cake horizontally into three layers. Brush each layer with syrup. Spread first layer with half the ricotta. Spread the second layer with remaining ricotta. Ice with Incredible Chocolate Icing. Decorate with pine nuts or pistachios.

*An authentic Sicilian dessert. As they say in Italy, "O pancia mia! Fatti capanna!" (Oh, belly of mine! Make yourself a warehouse!)*

# Mirror Glaze

| | |
|---|---|
| ½ cup *(125 mL)* strong coffee<br>⅓ cup *(75 mL)* sugar | Combine in heavy saucepan and heat until sugar is melted. |
| 6 oz. *(170 g)* semi-sweet chocolate | Chop coarsely and add. |
| 2 Tbsp. *(30 mL)* light corn syrup | Add and boil for 5 minutes, then remove from heat. |
| 2 Tbsp. *(30 mL)* butter<br>2 Tbsp. *(30 mL)* coffee-flavoured liqueur | Add butter and liqueur and beat until mixture thickens. |

Spread on cake immediately. Makes just under 1½ cups *(375 mL)*.

*This stores well. Just reheat in double boiler and beat again.*

# Zuccotto Florentino

Make sponge cake as in Cassata (page 26) but bake in round 9″ (*23 cm*) pan.

Make Cointreau Syrup as in Cassata (page 26).

## Filling #1

| | |
|---|---|
| 1 tsp. (*5 mL*) gelatine<br>1 Tbsp. (*15 mL*) cold water | Dissolve in double boiler over hot water and stir to melt. |
| 1½ cups (*375 mL*) heavy cream<br>¼ cup (*50 mL*) icing sugar | Beat until soft peaks form. Then add gelatine mixture and continue beating until firm peaks form. |
| 3 oz. (*85 g*) semi-sweet chocolate, coarsely chopped<br>2 Tbsp. (*30 mL*) Cointreau or orange liqueur | Add. |

## Filling #2

| | |
|---|---|
| 1½ cups (*375 mL*) heavy cream | Beat until stiff peaks form. |
| 6 oz. (*170 g*) semi-sweet chocolate, melted and cooled slightly | Add chocolate to cream in slow stream. |
| 2 Tbsp. (*30 mL*) brandy | Add. |
| ½ cup (*125 mL*) chopped almonds, toasted | Fold in. |

Mirror Glaze (page 27)

## To Assemble

Line 2½ qt. (*2½ L*) bowl with plastic wrap. Divide cake horizontally into three layers. Set top of cake, cut side up, into bowl. Brush with syrup, using pastry brush. Spread Cointreau cream (Filling #1) over cake. Place middle layer of cake over cream. Brush with syrup.

Spread with chocolate cream (Filling #2). Brush cut side of final layer with remaining syrup and press against chocolate cream. Chill for three hours or overnight. Top with glaze. Chill. Remove from refrigerator 15 minutes before serving.

*An awe-inspiring presentation. Don't tell your guests how simple it is to make.*

# Mocha Crinkles

Preheat oven to 350°F (*180°C*).

| | |
|---|---|
| 2 oz. (*60 g*) unsweetened chocolate<br>1½ cups (*375 mL*) semi-sweet chocolate chips<br>¼ cup (*50 mL*) butter | Melt together, stirring until smooth. Set aside. |
| 2 eggs<br>¾ cup (*175 mL*) sugar | Beat together until mixture is thick and pale. |
| 1 Tbsp. (*15 mL*) instant espresso powder<br>1 tsp. (*5 mL*) vanilla | Beat into sugar mixture. |
| | Fold in chocolate mixture. |
| ¼ cup (*50 mL*) flour<br>¼ tsp. (*1 mL*) baking powder | Combine and fold in. |
| ⅓ cup (*75 mL*) chocolate chips | Fold in. |
| | Let batter rest for 15 minutes. |

Drop by tablespoons (*15-mL spoons*) onto parchment-lined cookie sheets, 2″ (*5 cm*) apart. Bake for 9–12 minutes or until puffed, shiny and cracked-looking on top. Don't overbake. Cool completely. Makes about 2 dozen.

*Chocolate and caffeine cravings are both satisfied by this simple recipe.*

# White Chocolate Banana Cake

Preheat oven to 350°F (*180°C*).

| | |
|---|---|
| 1 cup (*250 mL*) butter | Melt. Cool until just warm. |
| 1¼ cups (*300 mL*) sugar | Beat in well. |
| 2 eggs<br>1 tsp. (*5 mL*) vanilla<br>3 Tbsp. (*45 mL*) brandy<br>or rum | Add to sugar mixture and beat on high speed for 5 minutes, until pale and thick. |
| 2–2¼ cups/*550 mL* (about 5) mashed bananas | Add to above and beat until well mixed. |
| 2¾ cups (*675 mL*) flour<br>1¼ tsp. (*6 mL*) baking soda | Combine and slowly beat on low speed to mix. |
| 8 oz. (*250 g*) white chocolate, chopped<br>1 cup (*250 mL*) pecans (or walnuts), lightly toasted<br>1¼ cups (*300 mL*) shredded coconut | Stir in. |

Pour into prepared 10–12 cup (*2–2.5 L*) prepared bundt pan or two loaf pans. Bake for about 1 hour and 15 minutes or until cake tests done. Cover with foil if cake is browning too much. Cool 15 minutes. Remove cake from pan. Cool thoroughly, then cover with White Chocolate Glaze if desired.

*A great way to get your potassium! The coconut and white chocolate give a new lease on life to those overripe bananas in your fruit bowl.*

# White Chocolate Glaze

12 oz. (*340 g*) white chocolate
¼ cup (*50 mL*) very hot water }

Melt chocolate in water and stir vigorously until creamy. Pour over cooled cake.

Refrigerate cake to set glaze. Serve at room temperature.

*A charming restaurateur in Nice parted willingly with the recipe for this simple glaze, which oozes seductively over cakes and loaves.*

# Black Velvet Tarte

1 fully baked 10″ (*25 cm*) tarte shell (use either Almond Crunch Crust, p. 78, or Chocolate Crust, p. 33)

12 oz. (*375 g*) semi-sweet chocolate

Melt and set aside.

½ cup (*125 mL*) heavy cream
½ cup (*125 mL*) half and half (light cream)
⅓ cup (*75 mL*) sour cream
1 egg yolk }

Combine and cook over medium heat in heavy saucepan, stirring constantly, until just bubbling at edges. Remove from heat and whisk slowly into melted chocolate.

¾ tsp. (*3 mL*) vanilla

Add.

Press through sieve into tarte shell. Refrigerate until set, 2–3 hours.

*The texture and taste are as smooth, sensuous and seductive as the name suggests. Proceed with caution!*

## Mocha Crème Caramel

Preheat oven to 325°F (*160°C*).

⅔ cup (*150 mL*) sugar
3 Tbsp. (*45 mL*) water

Stir together over medium heat in small heavy saucepan until sugar dissolves, then boil without stirring until deep golden (wash down sugar crystals that form on sides of pan with brush dipped in cold water).

Immediately divide amount into six ½-cup (*125-mL*) or four 1-cup (*250-mL*) custard cups, covering bottoms only. Set aside.

1½ cups (*375 mL*) heavy cream
½ cup (*125 mL*) 2% or whole milk
¼ cup (*50 mL*) sugar

Combine and bring to boil in heavy saucepan. Whisk to dissolve sugar. Remove from heat.

4 oz. (*115 g*) milk chocolate, chopped
3 Tbsp. (*45 mL*) instant espresso powder
½ tsp. (*2 mL*) vanilla

Stir into hot cream until mixture is smooth.

3 egg yolks
1 whole egg

Whisk together, then whisk into chocolate mixture.

Pour mixture into cups, dividing evenly. Place cups in pan filled with hot water to one half the depth of the cups. Bake until just set, about 30 minutes. Cool, then chill.

*Flip out to serve. (Your guests will flip out too!) Perfect at Passover.*

# Recipes

# Double Dark Chocolate Truffle Tarte

## Chocolate Crust

| | |
|---|---|
| ¾ cup (*175 mL*) flour<br>⅓ cup (*75 mL*) sugar<br>⅓ cup (*75 mL*) cocoa } | Combine in food processor. |
| ⅓ cup (*75 mL*) cold butter | Cut in until mixture is in fine crumbs. |
| 1 tsp. (*5 mL*) vanilla | Add. |
| up to 2 tsp. (*10 mL*) ice water | Add water drop by drop, enough to bind. Roll into ball, flatten and refrigerate 20 minutes. |
| | Preheat oven to 375°F (*190°C*). |

Remove dough from refrigerator. Roll out to fit 10″–11″ (*25cm–28cm*) tarte pan. Prick all over gently. Bake for 12 minutes or until set. (Tarte shell will not be baked again.)

## Filling

| | |
|---|---|
| 1½ cups (*375 mL*)<br>heavy cream | Scald. |
| 10 oz. (*300 g*) semi-sweet chocolate chips | Stir cream into chocolate as gently as possible, to melt. |
| 1½ Tbsp. (*25 mL*) Bailey's Irish Cream or liqueur of your choice } | Add to mixture. |

Press through fine sieve into cooled tarte shell. Refrigerate at least 2 hours until firm. Sift unsweetened cocoa over top to decorate before serving.

*You're really ahead of the game if you have unbaked crusts on hand in the freezer. Then it's just minutes to create this very serious chocolate lovers' dessert.*

# Caramel Macadamia Cognac Tarte

1 fully baked 9" *(23 cm)*
tarte shell

1 cup *(250 mL)* sugar
⅔ cup *(150 mL)* water }
Combine and heat in small, heavy saucepan on low heat. Stir to dissolve sugar.

Increase heat to boil mixture. Do not stir until mixture turns deep amber, about 12 minutes. (Brush sugar crystals from sides of pan with wet pastry brush.) Remove from heat.

1 cup *(250 mL)* heavy cream
½ cup *(125 mL)* butter }
Add to sugar mixture and stir.

2 egg yolks or
1 whole egg, whisked
Whisk some hot liquid into egg, then return to caramel. Cook over low heat until colour deepens and mixture is slightly thick, approximately 3 minutes.

1–2 tsp. *(5–10 mL)* cognac
Stir in. Cool 5 minutes.

⅔–1 cup *(150–250 mL)*
unsalted macadamia nuts
Sprinkle evenly into tarte shall.

Sieve hot caramel mixture over nuts.

Chill, then cover with Mirror Glaze (p. 27) or Lazy Gourmet Glaze (p. 46).

*This dessert is a perfect combination of all of our favourites—caramel, chocolate and macadamia nuts.*

# Recipes

## Bittersweet Hot Fudge Sauce

| | |
|---|---|
| 1 cup (*250 mL*) sugar <br> ¾ cup (*175 mL*) cocoa <br> 1½ Tbsp. (*25 mL*) instant coffee | Combine in saucepan. |
| ½ cup (*125 mL*) heavy cream | Add and blend to a smooth paste. |
| ½ cup (*125 mL*) heavy cream | Add and blend well. |
| | Place mixture over medium heat and stir until sugar is dissolved. |
| 2 Tbsp. (*30 mL*) butter | Add butter. Cook, stirring, for 6–7 minutes. Remove from heat at once. |

Keep chilled and reheat to serve. This sauce also freezes well.

## Chocolate Fudge

| | |
|---|---|
| ⅔ cup (*150 mL*) cocoa <br> 3 cups (*750 mL*) sugar <br> 1½ cups (*375 mL*) heavy cream | Combine in heavy saucepan, mixing well, then on medium heat bring to a rolling boil. Now reduce heat (DO NOT STIR!) and cook until mixture reaches 234°F (*112°C*) — soft ball stage. |
| | Cool to lukewarm (110°F/ *34°C*). Now beat until thick. (This will not take very long.) |

Spread fudge in an 8″ (*20 cm*) pan and when cool, cut into squares.

*Don't be afraid to use a candy thermometer.*

# Chocolate Mousse Trifle

This extraordinary trifle was chosen the Best Tasting Dessert, professional category, at Vancouver's first Chocolate Festival. There are six steps to its preparation:

1   Make the cake a day ahead if possible.
2   Now make the mousse.
3   Then whip the cream and divide it in half.
4   Measure the toasted nuts.
5   Combine milk and liqueur.
6   Assemble and enjoy.

Preheat oven to 325°F (*160°C*).

## Chocolate Cake

| | |
|---|---|
| 2 medium eggs<br>1 cup (*250 mL*) sugar<br>2 Tbsp. (*30 mL*) soft butter<br>1 cup (*250 mL*) oil<br>½ cup (*125 mL*) cocoa, packed<br>½ cup (*125 mL*) buttermilk<br>1 tsp. (*5 mL*) vanilla | Combine in this order. |
| 2¼ cups (*550 mL*) flour<br>1½ tsp. (*7 mL*) baking powder<br>1½ tsp. (*7 mL*) baking soda | Sift and add to above. |
| 1 cup (*250 mL*) boiling water | Fold in. Then fold mixture into two prepared, round 8″ or 9″ (*20–23 cm*) pans and bake for 25 minutes. |

## Mousse

| | |
|---|---|
| New Unbelievable Chocolate Mousse (page 13) | Prepare using 3 tbsp. (*45 mL*) Amaretto liqueur. |

# Recipes

## Cream

| | |
|---|---|
| 1 qt. (*1 L*) heavy cream<br>½ cup (*125 mL*) icing sugar | Beat together until soft peaks form. Divide cream mixture in half. |
| ¼ cup (*50 mL*) cold strong coffee<br>1 Tbsp. (*15 mL*) instant coffee<br>1 Tbsp. (*15 mL*) coffee liqueur | Combine, add to one-half of the cream and beat. Then set aside both bowls. |

## Nuts and Liqueur

| | |
|---|---|
| 1 cup (*250 mL*) toasted nuts | Your favourite: hazelnuts, pecans, almonds or walnuts. |
| 1 cup (*250 mL*) milk<br>⅓ cup (*75 mL*) coffee or chocolate liqueur | Combine. |

1 cup (*250 mL*) Bittersweet
Fudge Sauce
(page 35)

## To Assemble

In a 4 qt. (*4 L*) glass bowl: Spoon some cream on bottom of bowl; dunk some cake in milk mixture and place over cream. Drizzle on one-third fudge sauce. Sprinkle some nuts on this, then pour half the mousse over the cake. Add more cake and more nuts; then add coffee-flavoured cream and more fudge sauce. Add remaining cake, more nuts, and rest of mousse. Top with remaining cream and fudge sauce and sprinkle with nuts.

*A seduction of liqueur-drenched cake and creams. Delightfully decadent.*

# *Chocolate*

## Homemade Chocolate Mints

Preheat oven to 350°F (*180°C*).

| | |
|---|---|
| 6 oz. (*170 g*) unsweetened chocolate<br>¾ cup (*175 mL*) butter | In double boiler melt over hot water. |
| 3 eggs<br>1½ cups (*375 mL*) sugar<br>½ tsp. (*2 mL*) peppermint extract | In separate bowl beat eggs until frothy. Add sugar, extract and then stir into chocolate mixture. |
| ¾ cup (*175 mL*) flour | Add and mix well. |

Pour into buttered 9″ × 13″ (*23 cm* × *33 cm*) pan and bake for 20–25 minutes until finger does not leave indent. DO NOT OVERBAKE.

| | |
|---|---|
| 2 cups (*500 mL*) icing sugar<br>4 Tbsp. (*60 mL*) milk<br>2 tsp. (*10 mL*) peppermint extract<br>Green food colouring | Mix well and spread over base. |
| 2 oz. (*60 g*) semi–sweet chocolate | Melt and drizzle over mints. Cut into thin bars or squares. |

*No commercial chocolate mints can match these for richness and flavour. Serve after a meal or on festive occasions. They freeze beautifully.*

## Tout Sweet Cappuccino Truffles

| | |
|---|---|
| 8 oz. (*250 g*) semi–sweet chocolate<br>3½ Tbsp. (*50 mL*) butter | Melt and remove from heat. Beat together until blended. |
| 2 tsp. (*10 mL*) instant coffee | Add. |
| ¼ cup (*50 mL*) evaporated milk | Add. |
| | Chill until set. Roll into balls (makes about 20). Freeze for 1 hour. |

4 oz. (*115 g*) white chocolate, melted

Dip frozen truffles into white chocolate. Remove quickly to prevent dark chocolate from melting into white.

Chill until ready to serve.

*Our friend Anna De Flores of Gastown's Tout Sweet is famous for her truffles. She has graciously permitted us to pass on this recipe — our favourite.*

# Black Bottom Cupcakes

Preheat oven to 350°F (*180°C*).

¼ cup (*50 mL*) cocoa
1 cup (*250 mL*) sugar
1 tsp. (*5 mL*) baking soda
1½ cups (*375 mL*) flour

Combine in this order.

1 cup (*250 mL*) water
⅓ cup (*75 mL*) light oil
2 Tbsp. (*30 mL*) white vinegar
1 tsp. (*5 mL*) vanilla

Mix together until blended, then slowly add to the above.

Line cupcake tins with paper containers and fill each two-thirds full.

½ cup (*125 mL*) soft cream cheese
1 egg
¼ cup (*50 mL*) sugar

Blend well and drop by spoonfuls onto chocolate cupcake bases.

1 cup (*250 mL*) chocolate chips

Sprinkle each cupcake with chocolate chips.

Bake for 25 minutes. Yield: one dozen.

*A coveted Lazy Gourmet recipe.*

# Chocolate

## Poppyseed Bundt Cake

Preheat oven to 350°F (*180°C*).

| | |
|---|---|
| ½ cup (*125 mL*) poppyseeds<br>1 cup (*250 mL*) buttermilk<br>or yogurt | Combine and let soak for at least ½ hour. Set aside. |
| ½ cup (*125 mL*) butter<br>1¼ cups (*300 mL*) sugar | Cream until fluffy. |
| 4 egg yolks | Beat into butter/sugar mixture one at a time. |
| 2 tsp. (*10 mL*) vanilla | Add and beat well. |
| 2½ cups (*525 mL*) flour<br>2 tsp. (*10 mL*) baking powder<br>1 tsp. (*5 mL*) baking soda | Combine and add alternately with poppyseed mixture to butter/sugar mixture. |
| 4 egg whites | Beat until stiff, then fold in. |
| ¼ cup (*50 mL*) cocoa<br>¼ cup (*50 mL*) cinnamon<br>1 Tbsp. (*15 mL*) sugar | Combine and stir carefully into mixture. |
| ¾ cup (*175 mL*) chocolate chips (minis are best) | Stir in. |

Bake in greased bundt pan for 1 hour. Cool 5 minutes before turning out.

*Perfect for an afternoon coffee klatch. Serve with cappuccino.*

# Recipes

## Chocolate "Pudding Cake"

Preheat oven to 375°F (*190°C*).

| | |
|---|---|
| 4 oz. (*115 g*) unsweetened chocolate<br>½ cup (*125 mL*) unsalted butter | Melt together in double boiler, then cool until tepid. |
| 3 eggs<br>1 cup (*250 mL*) sugar | Beat together until thick and light yellow (2–3 minutes). |
| | On low speed, beat in chocolate to blend. |
| 1 Tbsp. (*15 mL*) liqueur (your favourite) | Add and blend in. |

Pour into parchment-lined loaf pan, then set in another pan filled with hot, not boiling, water to one half the depth of the loaf pan.

Bake for 40–45 minutes, until tester comes out with moist crumbs. Cool.

*or*

Pour mixture into prebaked 10″ (*25 cm*) tarte shell. Bake for 25 minutes or until tester comes out with moist crumbs. Serve with Raspberry Sauce (p. 63) and Crème Anglaise (p. 63).

*Not a mousse, not a cake, not really a pudding, this is a slice of pure heaven. A good choice for a Passover dessert, too.*

# Flan Crust (Press Style)

Preheat oven to 350°F (*180°C*).

| | |
|---|---|
| 1½ cups (*375 mL*) flour<br>1½ Tbsp. (*25 mL*) sugar } | Mix together. |
| ⅝ cup (*150 mL*) butter | Cut in butter until coarse crumbs form. |
| 1 egg yolk | Blend in. |
| 1 tsp. (*5 mL*) grated lemon<br>peel (optional)<br>Dash of brandy } | Add. |

Turn onto board and knead briefly (unnecessary if food processor has been used). Place in 10″–12″ (*25–30 cm*) flan pan and pat dough against bottom and sides. Partially bake for 25–30 minutes until golden. To fully bake, leave in for an additional 10 minutes. Use with your favourite flan recipe.

# Shortbread Crust (Press Style)

Preheat oven to 300°F (*150°C*).

| | |
|---|---|
| 1 cup (*250 mL*) unsalted butter<br>½ cup (*125 mL*) icing sugar<br>1½ tsp. (*7 mL*) vanilla<br>2 cups (*500 mL*) flour } | Combine and process in food processor until crumbly. Press into two flan pans or two 10″ (*25 cm*) tarte shells. |

Bake for 40–45 minutes or until golden. Doesn't shrink!

*Throw away your rolling pins! Here are two fabulous pastry crusts that require no tedious, anxiety-producing rolling.*

# Five-Minute Brownie Tarte

| | Preheat oven to 325°F (*160°C*). |
|---|---|
| 4 oz. (*115 g*) semi-sweet chocolate | Melt and set aside. |
| ½ cup (*125 mL*) butter<br>¾ cup (*175 mL*) sugar | Combine and beat well<br>(3 minutes to dissolve sugar). |
| 2 eggs<br>1 tsp. (*5 mL*) vanilla | Add to butter and sugar mixture.<br>Beat in well. |
| | Beat in melted chocolate on low speed. |
| ⅓ cup (*75 mL*) flour<br>¼ cup (*50 mL*) cocoa<br>¼ tsp. (*1 mL*) baking powder | Combine, then beat into mixture on low speed until blended. |

Pour into 9″ or 10″ (*23–25 cm*) pie plate that has been sprayed with no-stick cooking spray. Bake for 25 minutes or until *just* tests done; moist crumbs should adhere to toothpick.

*Guests coming with only 15 minutes' warning? Try serving wedges of this tarte with ice cream and/or hot fudge sauce for rave reviews! (You could sprinkle toasted nuts on top as well.)*

# Mocha Mousse Meringue Cake

Preheat oven to 250°F (*120°C*).

### Meringue

Trace four 8″ (*20-cm*) circles on cookie sheets lined with waxed or parchment paper (a standard salad plate can be used as a guide). Lightly sift icing sugar over paper.

4 Tbsp. (*60 mL*) instant coffee
2 tsp. (*10 mL*) hot water } Dissolve coffee in water.

2 cups (*500 mL*) icing sugar
6 Tbsp. (*90 mL*) cocoa } Sift together and set aside.

10 egg whites — In large bowl, beat until soft peaks form.

1⅓ cups (*325 mL*) sugar — Add to egg whites 1 Tbsp. (*15 mL*) at a time. Continue beating until stiff peaks form.

Beat in coffee mixture. Fold in cocoa mixture.

Make four meringue disks, using 1¼ cup (*300 mL*) of mixture for each, on the paper-lined cookie sheets, following circles traced earlier. Put extra meringue mixture into piping bag and pipe onto another cookie sheet in long tubes.

Bake until crisp (approximately 1 hour and 10 minutes). Break meringue tubes on cookie sheets into 3″ (*8 cm*) pieces once they are cool.

### Mousse

8 oz. (*250 g*) semi-sweet chocolate
4 oz. (*125 g*) bitter chocolate
1½ cups (*375 mL*) unsalted butter } Melt over hot water. Stir until smooth. Let cool.

¼ cup (*50 mL*) corn syrup

| | |
|---|---|
| 1 Tbsp. *(15 mL)* vanilla | Add to chocolate mixture. Set mixture aside. |
| ⅔ cup *(150 mL)* sugar<br>4 Tbsp. *(60 mL)* water } | Stir over low heat until sugar is dissolved. Boil 1 minute. |
| 8 egg whites | Beat until soft peaks form. Gradually, over a period of 5 minutes, beat in boiling syrup and continue to beat until cool. |
| | Fold ½ of egg-white mixture into chocolate. When incorporated, fold in remainder. |
| 1 cup *(250 mL)* heavy cream | Beat until soft peaks form. Fold into chocolate mixture. |
| | Refrigerate until just beginning to set. |

## To Assemble:

1. Put dollop of mousse in centre of platter to keep meringue from sliding. Divide rest of mousse into five portions.

2. Place a meringue disk on platter.

3. Top with one portion of mousse.

4. Continue to layer meringue disks and mousse.

5. Spread remaining mousse around sides.

6. Press broken pieces of meringue into mousse around cake, saving some to decorate top. Dust with icing sugar or cocoa.

*Wow your guests with this phenomenal French fantasy! It's well worth the time and effort, and it's really fun to make.*

# Chocolate

## White Chocolate Crème Anglaise

¼ cup (*50 mL*) sugar
Pinch of salt
5 egg yolks
2 Tbsp. (*30 mL*) fresh lemon juice

Combine in medium saucepan.

1 cup (*250 mL*) half and half (light cream), scalded

Whisk into above over medium heat and cook until thickened (about 8 minutes). Remove from heat.

1 Tbsp. (*15 mL*) vanilla

Add.

5 oz. (*150 g*) white chocolate, chopped into small pieces

Add to warm mixture and stir until melted. Strain through a fine sieve and refrigerate until ready to serve.

Makes about 1 cup (*250 mL*).

*Try serving with fresh fruit in summer or baked apples in winter.*

## The Lazy Gourmet Glaze

¼ cup (*50 mL*) butter
4 oz. (*115 g*) semi-sweet chocolate

Melt together.

2 Tbsp. (*30 mL*) heavy cream
1 Tbsp. (*15 mL*) coffee liqueur

Mix well and add to chocolate.

# PECANS

## Frosty Butter Pecan Mousse

Line a 4 cup (*1 L*) bowl or ring mould with plastic wrap.

2 egg whites
½ cup (*125 mL*) sugar

Using electric mixer, beat egg whites until soft peaks form. Add sugar gradually and beat until stiff peaks form.

2 egg yolks
1 tsp. (*5 mL*) vanilla

Beat well and carefully fold whites into yolks.

1 cup (*250 mL*) heavy cream

Beat until soft peaks form. Fold into egg mixture.

¾ cup (*175 mL*) toasted pecans, coarsely chopped
1½ oz. (*45 g*) unsweetened chocolate, finely chopped

Fold into above.

Bittersweet Hot Fudge Sauce (page 35) (optional)

Pour into ring mould and freeze until firm. Decorate with whole pecans or pour fudge sauce over mousse just before serving.

*A simple extravagance.*

# Pecan Glazed Torte

| | Preheat oven to 350°F *(180°C)*. |
|---|---|
| 6 oz. *(170 g)* semi-sweet chocolate | Melt and set aside. |
| ½ cup *(125 mL)* soft butter | Beat until very smooth. |
| ½ cup *(125 mL)* sugar | Gradually add to butter until mixture is fluffy. |
| 4 egg yolks | Beat into butter mixture one at a time. |
| | Add chocolate and blend. |
| 1 cup *(250 mL)* pecans, finely chopped <br> 4 Tbsp. *(60 mL)* flour } | Mix and add to above. |
| 4 egg whites | Beat until stiff and gently fold in. |

The Lazy Gourmet Glaze
(page 46)

Pour into prepared, round 9″ *(23 cm)* pan. Bake for 25 minutes. When cooled, place cake on rack over plate. Pour glaze over cake and tilt cake to edge glaze over sides. Decorate with pecans. Serve chilled.

*Although this torte is rich and dense, the lightness of the pecans gives it an almost ethereal quality.*

# The Quintessential Turtle

1½ cups (*375 mL*) whole pecans, toasted

Place on buttered cookie sheet in clumps of threes.

## Caramel

1 cup (*250 mL*) sugar
⅔ cup (*150 mL*) light corn syrup
⅔ cup (*150 mL*) light cream
dash salt
3 Tbsp. (*45 mL*) butter

In medium-sized saucepan, mix well and bring to a boil, stirring constantly.

⅓ cup (*75 mL*) light cream

When mixture starts to boil, add more cream and cook slowly until candy thermometer reads 246°F (*118°C*) (firm ball stage).

½ tsp. (*2 mL*) vanilla

Remove from heat and add vanilla.

Let cool for one minute. Mix well and, using two teaspoons — one for scooping, one for pushing — drop caramel onto pecans.

Let harden about 5 minutes.

4 oz. (*115 g*) semi-sweet chocolate, melted

Spread over caramel.

*This recipe was donated by a fiendish dentist!*

# Turtle Flan

Preheat oven to 400°F (*200°C*).

## Crust

| | |
|---|---|
| ⅓ cup (*75 mL*) cold butter<br>⅓ cup (*75 mL*) sugar | Cream together in food processor. |
| 2 egg yolks<br>½ tsp. (*2 mL*) vanilla | Add slowly while processing. |
| ⅔ cup (*150 mL*) flour | Stop machine and add. Do not overmix. |

Press into 10″ (*25 cm*) tarte shell or flan pan and bake until slightly golden (approximately 20 minutes).

## Filling

| | |
|---|---|
| | Reduce oven temperature to 350°F (*180°C*). |
| 2½ oz. (¼ cup/*50 mL*) semi-sweet chocolate | Melt. |
| 1½ Tbsp. (*25 mL*) butter<br>¼ cup (*50 mL*) sugar | Heat together to melt butter.<br>Add to melted chocolate. |
| 2 eggs | Whisk together, then whisk into chocolate mixture. |
| ⅕ cup (*50 mL*) flour | Blend in. |
| ½ cup (*125 mL*) pecans, chopped | Place in shell and pour filling over top. |
| | Bake for 15 minutes. |

## Caramel Topping

| | |
|---|---|
| ¼ cup (*50 mL*) heavy cream<br>1 Tbsp. (*15 mL*) corn syrup<br>2 Tbsp. (*30 mL*) butter | Boil together in saucepan for 1–2 minutes. |

½ cup (*125 mL*) sugar
½ tsp. (*2 mL*) vanilla

In another small, heavy saucepan, heat together until sugar is melted and mixture is liquid and golden. Add the boiling cream to the caramel and stir to combine. Mixture will "fizz" a bit—don't worry. Pour over the flan and let set in refrigerator.

*An updated version of those chewy, gooey candy turtles, dressed for elegance.*

# The Lazy Gourmet Pecan Pie

Preheat oven to 350°F (*180°C*).

1 unbaked 9″ (*23 cm*) pie shell
(page 24)

| | |
|---|---|
| 3 eggs | Beat eggs. |
| 1 cup (*250 mL*) brown sugar | Add sugar and mix. |
| ⅓ cup (*75 mL*) melted butter | Stir in. |
| 1 cup (*250 mL*) light corn syrup | Stir in. |
| ½ tsp. (*2 mL*) vanilla | Add. |
| 1⅓ cups (*325 mL*) pecans, toasted | Put pecans in pie shell. |
| | Pour filling over pecans. (They will rise to the top.) |

Bake for 45 minutes. Serve chilled or at room temperature with whipped cream.

*We've searched but can find no richer, more satisfying pecan pie recipe. Once you cut into it, you'll want to "even the edges" until it's all gone.*

# $250 Cookies

Preheat oven to 375°F (*190°C*).

| | |
|---|---|
| 1 cup (*250 mL*) butter<br>1 cup (*250 mL*) sugar<br>1 cup (*250 mL*) brown sugar | In large bowl, cream together well. |
| 2 eggs<br>1 tsp. (*5 mL*) vanilla | Add and cream. |
| 2 cups (*500 mL*) flour<br>1¾ cups (*425 mL*) powdered oatmeal (2½ cups/*625 mL* oatmeal pulverized in blender to fine powder)<br>1 tsp. (*5 mL*) baking powder<br>1 tsp. (*5 mL*) baking soda | Combine and mix with above. |
| 12 oz. (*350 g*) chocolate chips<br>4 oz. (*115 g*) milk chocolate, grated<br>1½ cups (*375 mL*) lightly toasted pecans | Add to dough. Stir to mix well. |

Scoop out with generous tablespoons (*15-mL spoons*) onto prepared cookie sheets. Bake for 10 minutes. Makes about 5 dozen.

*This is the original N-M cookie recipe, offered by a woman who actually paid $250 for it. You now owe us $235!*

# Pecan Shortbread Squares

Preheat oven to 350°F *(180°C)*.

| | |
|---|---|
| 1 cup *(250 mL)* butter<br>6 Tbsp. *(90 mL)* brown sugar<br>1 egg<br>1 tsp. *(5 mL)* lemon juice<br>3 cups *(750 mL)* flour | Blend well with food processor, electric mixer or hands. |

Press into 10″ × 15″ *(25 cm × 29 cm)* pan. Prick with fork. Bake for 20 minutes.

| | |
|---|---|
| 3 cups *(750 mL)* pecans | Spread pecans over shortbread. |
| 1½ cups *(375 mL)* butter<br>14 Tbsp. *(210 mL)* honey | In heavy saucepan, melt butter and honey together. |
| 1½ cups *(375 mL)* brown sugar | Add and bring to boil, cooking until dark brown, about 5–7 minutes, whisking continuously. Remove from heat. |
| 6 Tbsp. *(90 mL)* heavy cream | Add immediately. Mix and pour over pecans. |

Return shortbread to oven for 20 minutes. Cool to room temperature before cutting into squares.

*The caramel glues the pecans to the shortbread, creating a new version of an old southern favourite.*

 *Pecan*

## Pecan Rum Balls

1½ cups (*375 mL*) graham wafer crumbs
1 cup (*250 mL*) icing sugar
1 cup (*250 mL*) pecans, chopped
2½ Tbsp. (*40 mL*) cocoa
¼ cup (*50 mL*) corn syrup (light or dark)
¼ cup (*50 mL*) dark rum

Mix all ingredients until well blended. (Get your hands in there!)

Icing sugar, cocoa or melted chocolate

Roll into balls, then roll in icing sugar, cocoa *or* dip into melted chocolate. Makes about 3 dozen.

*They freeze well. Keep on hand in case of emergency, i.e., guests or chocolate attack.*

## Diddy's Delights

Preheat oven to 300°F (*150°C*).

1 cup (*250 mL*) soft butter
½ cup (*125 mL*) icing sugar
1½ Tbsp. (*25 mL*) vanilla
1¾ cups (*425 mL*) flour
1 cup (*250 mL*) pecans, finely chopped

Mix together well and drop by teaspoons onto ungreased cookie sheet.

Bake for 25 minutes. When cool, roll in icing sugar.

These freeze well, but don't roll in sugar until thawed. Makes 4 dozen.

*The easiest recipe in the book.*

# Pecan Fudge Pie

Preheat oven to 350°F (*180°C*).

Chocolate Crust (page 33)

## Fudge Filling

| | |
|---|---|
| 1¼ cups (*300 mL*) pecan halves | Spread over bottom of unbaked 9″ (*23 cm*) chocolate pie shell. |
| 3 eggs | Beat eggs. |
| ½ cup (*125 mL*) brown sugar<br>½ cup (*125 mL*) white sugar<br>1 cup (*250 mL*) light corn syrup | Add to eggs separately, mixing well after each addition. |
| 3 oz. (*85 g*) unsweetened chocolate<br>⅓ cup (*75 mL*) butter | Melt together and add. |
| 1 tsp. (*5 mL*) vanilla | Add. |

Pour filling into shell and bake for 40 minutes. Chill for 2 hours. Serve with unsweetened whipped cream.

*Worth every calorie.*

# Chocolate Glazed Pecan Pie

Chocolate Crust (page 33)

The Lazy Gourmet Pecan Pie Filling (page 51)   Pour into crust and bake for 45 minutes. Refrigerate. When chilled, spread with Fudge Glaze.

## Fudge Glaze

1 cup (*250 mL*) chocolate chips, melted and slightly cooled
1 Tbsp. (*15 mL*) brandy
2 Tbsp. (*30 mL*) soft butter   Whisk until well blended. Spread over pie and decorate with pecan halves.

*Our famous pecan pie filling sandwiched between two layers of chocolate fantasy.*

# Chewy, Chewy Chocolate Pecan Cookies

|  |  |
|---|---|
|  | Preheat oven to 350°F (*180°C*). |
| ⅔ lb. (*325 g*) butter | Cream. |
| 2 cups (*500 mL*) sugar | Add gradually to butter. |
| 2 eggs | Add one at a time, beating well. |
| ¼ tsp. (*1 mL*) vanilla | Stir in. |
| 2 cups (*500 mL*) flour<br>⅔ cup (*150 mL*) cocoa<br>1 tsp. (*5 mL*) baking powder<br>Pinch of salt | Sift together and add to above.<br>Do not overblend. |
| ⅔ cup (*150 mL*) chocolate chips<br>⅓ cup (*75 mL*) chopped pecans | Add. |

Drop by large tablespoons (*15-mL spoons*) onto prepared cookie sheet. Bake for 12 minutes. Makes about 20 large cookies.

*Don't overbake these cookies or they will lose the chewy quality that makes them such a hit.*

# Schmoo Torte

| | |
|---|---|
| | Preheat oven to 300°F (*150°C*). |
| ½ cup (*125 mL*) cake flour | Sift, remeasure and sift again. |
| 1 tsp. (*5 mL*) baking powder | Add to flour. Set aside. |
| 6 egg whites (use extra-large eggs) | Beat until almost stiff. |
| ¼ tsp. (*1 mL*) cream of tartar | Beat into egg whites. |
| ½ cup (*125 mL*) sugar | Add slowly to egg whites, beating until stiff. |
| | Fold in flour. |
| 6 egg yolks<br>½ cup (*125 mL*) sugar } | Beat together until very frothy. |
| | Fold yolk mixture into whites. |
| 1 tsp. (*5 mL*) vanilla | Add to yolk mixture. |
| 1 cup (*250 mL*) pecans, very finely chopped | Fold in. |
| | Bake in ungreased tube pan for 1 hour. Invert and cool before turning cake out. Cut cake into 3 layers. |
| 2 cups (*500 mL*) heavy cream<br>3 Tbsp. (*45 mL*) icing sugar<br>1 tsp. (*5 mL*) vanilla } | Beat until stiff peaks form. Spread whipped cream between layers and over top and sides. |
| | Serve with Caramel Sauce (p. 116). |

*What is a schmoo? Who knows, but we do know that its origin is Winnipeg—and that we love this cake!*

# Columbus Circles

| | |
|---|---|
| ½ cup (*125 mL*) flour<br>½ cup (*125 mL*) cornmeal<br>1 tsp. (*5 mL*) baking powder } | Combine. |
| ⅔ cup (*150 mL*) raisins<br>¾ cup (*175 mL*) chocolate chunks<br>1 cup (*250 mL*) toasted pecan pieces } | Stir into flour mixture. |
| ¾ cup (*175 mL*) butter<br>¾ tsp. (*3 mL*) cinnamon<br>¾ tsp. (*3 mL*) crushed anise seed } | Cream together 2 minutes. |
| ⅔ cup (*150 mL*) sugar | Add to butter mixture and beat 1–2 minutes to dissolve. |
| 1 egg<br>½ tsp (*2 mL*) vanilla } | Add to butter/sugar mixture and beat until well blended. |
| | Add dry ingredients to butter mixture, mixing thoroughly. |

Form into two 2″ × 12″ (*5 cm × 30 cm*) logs and wrap tightly with plastic wrap. Freeze until firm (about 1 hour).

Thaw for 5 minutes, then slice into ½″ (*1 cm*) rounds. Place on buttered cookie sheet 3″ (*8 cm*) apart. Bake at 350°F (*180°C*) for 12–14 minutes. Cool. Makes 2–3 dozen.

*The cornmeal and anise combine to give these cookies a wonderful, yet subtle, European texture and flavour.*

# HAZELNUTS

## Hazelnut Truffles

6 oz. (*170 g*) chocolate chips,
melted
2 Tbsp. (*30 mL*) brandy
2 Tbsp. (*30 mL*) light corn
syrup
⅔ cup (*150 mL*) icing sugar
½ cup (*125 mL*) hazelnuts,
toasted and crushed

Mix together and form into
balls. Chill well.

4 oz. (*115 g*) semi-sweet
chocolate, melted
⅛ tsp. (*0.5 mL*) paraffin wax
(optional)

Dip truffles in chocolate *or* roll
in sifted cocoa.

*or* cocoa

*So simple, this frequently requested recipe can be prepared in a few minutes.*

# Frozen Hazelnut Soufflé

|  |  |
|---|---|
|  | Prepare 8", 2 qt. (*20 cm, 2 L*) soufflé dish. Make a collar by cutting a piece of foil long enough to overlap around dish. Oil the part that will be inside. The foil should extend 4" (*10 cm*) above edge of dish. |
| 1¾ cups (*425 mL*) sugar<br>1 cup (*250 mL*) water | Stir together in small saucepan. Let boil without stirring for 5 minutes. |
| 9 egg yolks | Beat with electric mixer (using large bowl) at medium speed until lemon coloured. |
|  | Increase speed to high and slowly add sugar syrup. Continue to beat until cool and stiff. |
| 3 cups (*750 mL*) heavy cream | Beat until stiff, then fold all but ½ cup (*125 mL*) into egg mixture. |
| 1 cup (*250 mL*) hazelnuts, toasted and chopped<br>4 Tbsp. (*60 mL*) Frangelico liqueur | Add. |

Spoon into soufflé dish. Decorate with remaining whipped cream. Freeze for 6–8 hours or overnight. Serve while frozen.

*Serious competition for the best ice cream you've ever had and you don't need an ice cream maker.*

# *Hazelnut*

## Hazelnut Brownie Tarte with Raspberry Sauce or Crème Anglaise

### Pastry

| | |
|---|---|
| 1 cup *(250 mL)* flour<br>¼ cup *(50 mL)* brown sugar<br>3 Tbsp. *(45 mL)* cocoa<br>½ cup *(125 mL)* well-chilled butter<br>2 Tbsp. *(30 mL)* milk<br>1 tsp. *(5 mL)* vanilla | Using food processor, or pastry cutter, combine and mix until well blended. |
| | Press into prepared 11″ *(28 cm)* ring flan pan. |

### Filling

| | |
|---|---|
| 3 oz. *(85 g)* unsweetened chocolate<br>3 oz. *(85 g)* semi-sweet chocolate | Melt together in double boiler. Remove from heat. |
| ½ cup *(125 mL)* butter | Add butter 1 Tbsp. *(15 mL)* at a time until blended. |
| 1½ cups *(375 mL)* sugar | Add. |
| 3 eggs, beaten | Add eggs slowly, blending well. |
| 2 tsp. *(10 mL)* vanilla<br>¾ cups *(175 mL)* hazelnuts, toasted and coarsely chopped | Add vanilla and hazelnuts. |
| ¾ cup *(175 mL)* flour | Add and blend well. |

Pour into unbaked tarte shell. Bake for 25–30 minutes, until toothpick comes out clean. Be careful not to overbake. Serve with Raspberry Sauce or Crème Anglaise.

*A down-home brownie served with the elegance of a French dessert. To be absolutely outrageous, serve with both sauces, a spoonful on either side of each slice.*

# Recipes

## Raspberry Sauce

10 oz. (*280 g*) frozen raspberries *or* 2 cups (*500 mL*) fresh raspberries
1 Tbsp. (*15 mL*) kirsch
4 Tbsp. (*60 mL*) sugar

Process in blender or food processor until smooth. If desired, press through sieve to remove seeds.

For a thicker sauce, heat raspberries until mixture boils. Simmer for 30 seconds. Remove from heat and process in blender.

## Crème Anglaise

3 cups (*750 mL*) milk

Heat milk in top of double boiler over boiling water until very hot.

5 egg yolks
⅓ cup (*75 mL*) sugar
1½ Tbsp. (*25 mL*) flour

Mix in a bowl.

Add milk to egg mixture, stirring with a wire whisk. Return to top of double boiler and cook over simmering water until thickened, stirring constantly.

Cool by placing pot in cold water.

# Hazelnut Torte

| | Preheat oven to 350°F (*180°C*). |
|---|---|
| 7 egg whites | In large bowl, beat until frothy. |
| ⅓ cup (*75 mL*) sugar | Add very slowly to egg whites, beating until stiff peaks form. |
| 7 egg yolks | In another bowl, beat until very light. |
| ⅓ cup (*75 mL*) sugar<br>1 tsp. (*5 mL*) vanilla | Add to yolks and beat until thick and lemon coloured. |
| 1¼ cups (*300 mL*) hazelnuts, toasted and ground<br>3 Tbsp. (*45 mL*) graham cracker crumbs<br>1 tsp. (*5 mL*) baking powder<br>dash of salt | Combine and fold into yolks. |
| | Add yolk mixture to whites. |
| | Pour into three round 8″ or 9″ (*20–23 cm*) pans which have been lined with waxed paper *or* onto a waxed paper-lined 10″ × 15″ (*25 cm × 29 cm*) sheet. |

Bake for 15–18 minutes or until cake springs back when lightly touched. Be careful not to overcook. Cool. (If cookie sheet is used, cut into three equal pieces.)

Incredible Chocolate Icing (page 10) *or* Chocolate Buttercream (page 65)

Fill with flavoured whipped cream and ice with Incredible Chocolate Icing. Or, for an extra indulgence, fill and ice with Chocolate Buttercream. Chill for at least one hour. Use serrated knife to cut.

Cointreau Fudge Cake with Cointreau Icing (pages 8,9)

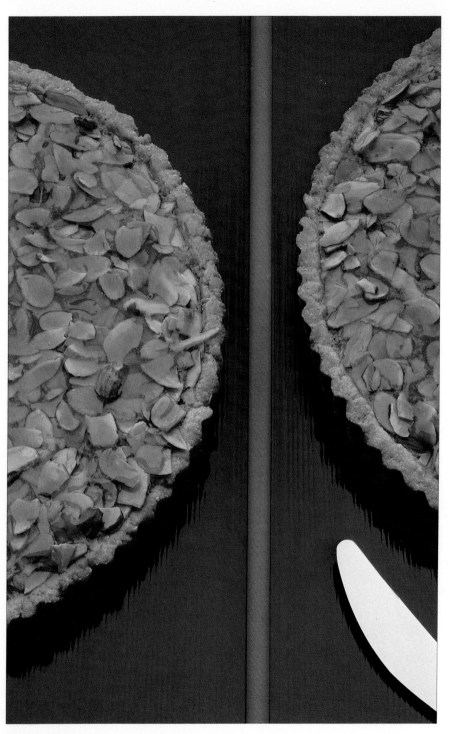

Almond Glazed Tarte (page 83)

Cassata with pine nut garnish (page 26)

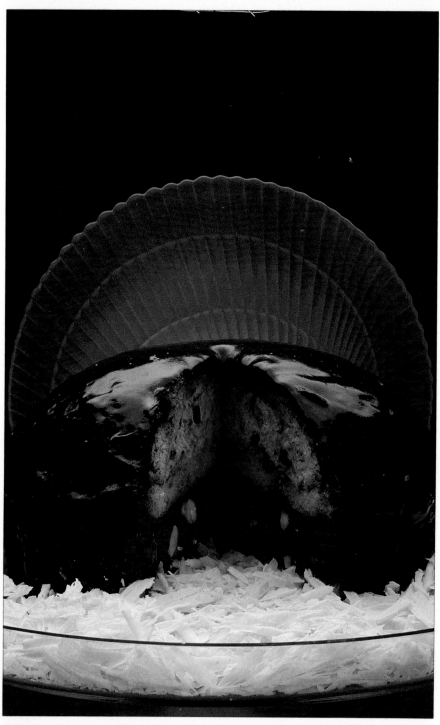

Zuccotto Florentino with slivers of white chocolate (page 28)

The Lazy Gourmet Pecan Pie (page 51)

Chocolate Glazed Pecan Pie with Chocolate Crust (page 56)

Lynnie's Baklava (page 93) and Frozen Hazelnut Soufflé (page 61)

Money-Back Guarantee Brownies (page 100) with Incredible Chocolate Icing (page 10), Homemade Chocolate Mints (page 38), Pecan Shortbread Squares (page 53), Diddy's Delights (page 54)

# Chocolate Buttercream

1 cup (*250 mL*) sugar
⅓ cup (*75 mL*) water

Combine in small heavy saucepan, cover and bring to boil. Boil for 2 minutes and remove cover. Boil to 240°F (*112°C*) — soft ball stage.

8 egg yolks

In bowl, using electric mixer, beat yolks on high speed until thick.

Reduce speed to medium and gradually pour in hot syrup.

Return to high speed and beat until mixture is cool.

1½ cups (*375 mL*) soft unsalted butter

Begin adding, 1 Tbsp. (*15 mL*) at a time until all butter is added.

6 oz. (*170 g*) unsweetened chocolate, melted and slightly cooled
1 tsp. (*5 mL*) vanilla

Add chocolate and vanilla.

# Hazelnut Fudge Torte

Preheat oven to 350°F (180°C).

⅔ cup (*150 mL*) hazelnuts, toasted and ground
¼ cup (*50 mL*) flour
1½ Tbsp. (*25 mL*) ground coffee beans
} Combine and set aside.

1 cup (*250 mL*) butter
7 oz. (*200 g*) semi-sweet chocolate
¾ cup (*175 mL*) sugar
} Melt butter and chocolate and let cool for a couple of minutes, then add sugar.

1½ Tbsp. (*25 mL*) coffee liqueur
4 eggs
} Mix well and add to chocolate mixture.

Now add dry ingredients.

Bake in prepared, round 9″ (*23 cm*) pan (or springform pan) for 25 minutes. Do not overbake. Cool, then chill.

The Lazy Gourmet Glaze
(page 46)

Place cake on rack with plate underneath. Pour glaze over top and gently spoon over sides. Decorate with 8–10 whole hazelnuts, toasted.

*This torte is best when chilled for a couple of days. It freezes well, so that you can make it ahead and glaze it the day you serve it.*

# Hazelnut Sauce

| | |
|---|---|
| 1¾ cups (*425 mL*) half and half (light cream), scalded<br>¾ cup (*175 mL*) toasted, blanched hazelnuts | Process in blender or food processor until smooth, then bring to a simmer in medium saucepan. Remove from heat. |
| 5 egg yolks<br>¼ cup (*50 mL*) sugar<br>¼ tsp. (*1 mL*) vanilla<br>Pinch of salt | Combine in separate medium saucepan. Press as much hot nut mixture as possible through sieve and whisk in. Cook over medium heat until custard is thick. Do not let boil. Remove from heat. Whisk until cool. Press through sieve again. |
| 2 Tbsp. (*30 mL*) Frangelico liqueur | Add. |
| | Cover and refrigerate until ready to serve. |

*Served over an uniced brownie with a scoop of ice cream, this is a dessert that memories are made of.*

# Chocolate Frangelico Cheesecake

Preheat oven to 350°F (*180°C*).

Chocolate Crust (page 14)     Press into 9″ or 10″ (*23–25 cm*) springform pan.

## Filling

2 cups (*500 mL*) soft cream cheese
½ cup (*125 mL*) sugar
4 oz. (*115 g*) semi-sweet chocolate, melted and slightly cooled
1 oz. (*30 g*) unsweetened chocolate, melted and slightly cooled
2 large eggs
½ cup (*125 mL*) sour cream
2 Tbsp. (*30 mL*) Frangelico liqueur

Beat with electric mixer, adding ingredients in this order and then beating for 10 minutes on medium-high speed.

Pour over crust and bake for 30–35 minutes until firm to touch. Cool, then chill 2–3 hours.

## Topping

1 cup (*250 mL*) heavy cream     Beat until *soft* peaks form.

2 Tbsp. (*30 mL*) icing sugar
2 Tbsp. (*30 mL*) Frangelico liqueur

Combine and spread over cake.

4 Tbsp. (*60 mL*) hazelnuts, toasted and crushed
chocolate curls

Decorate with crushed nuts and chocolate curls (page 5).

*Decorative curls made with Belgian hazelnut chocolate are easier to work with than regular chocolate.*

# ALMONDS

## Almond Ginger Florentines

Preheat oven to 350°F (*180°C*).

⅓ cup (*75 mL*) sugar
½ cup (*125 mL*) heavy cream

In heavy saucepan, cook together over medium heat to dissolve sugar. Bring to a boil, then reduce heat and simmer 3 minutes.

1 Tbsp. (*15 mL*) unsalted butter
3 Tbsp. (*45 mL*) flour
½ cup (*125 mL*) finely chopped or grated candied ginger
1¼ cups (*300 mL*) sliced almonds, toasted

Add to sweetened cream. Stir on low heat for 3 minutes.

Drop batter from a teaspoon (*5-mL spoon*) onto parchment-lined cookie sheets 2–3" (*5–8 cm*) apart. Bake for 8–10 minutes until golden. Cool thoroughly before removing from cookie sheets. Makes 2–3 dozen.

*The sweet ginger has a bite that makes these cookies explode with flavour.*

# Chocolate Almond Gateau

Preheat oven to 350°F (*180°C*).

| | |
|---|---|
| 1 cup (*250 mL*) soft butter | Cream. |
| 1 cup (*250 mL*) sugar | Add gradually. |
| 5 egg yolks | Beat in one at a time. |
| 4 oz. (*115 g*) semi-sweet chocolate<br>4 oz. (*115 g*) unsweetened chocolate | Melt chocolate; let cool and pour into yolk mixture. |
| 1 cup (*250 mL*) flour<br>6 Tbsp. (*90 mL*) milk | Add flour and milk alternately, stirring after each addition. |
| 1 tsp. (*5 mL*) vanilla<br>2 tsp. (*10 mL*) Amaretto liqueur | Stir in. |
| 1½ cups (*375 mL*) almonds, toasted and ground | Add. |
| 5 egg whites | Beat until stiff peaks form. Fold one-third egg white mixture into chocolate, then gently fold in the rest. |

Pour into shallow round 14″ (*38 cm*) pan lined with waxed paper. Bake for 25 minutes. Top should be firm when touched. But don't overbake! Remove carefully from oven and chill 2–3 hours before icing.

## Truffle Icing Glaze

| | |
|---|---|
| 8 oz. (*250 g*) semi-sweet chocolate<br>6 Tbsp. (*90 mL*) milk<br>6 Tbsp. (*90 mL*) butter | Melt in top of double boiler and let cool slightly. |

1¾ cups (*425 mL*) icing sugar, sifted
½ tsp. (*2 mL*) almond extract
2 tsp. (*10 mL*) Amaretto liqueur
} Beat into chocolate mixture.

Gently spread over top and sides of gateau. Decorate with slivered toasted almonds.

*A gateau to die for. Choose your dinner guests carefully.*

# Tropical Macaroons

Preheat oven to 350°F (*180°C*).

3 cups (*750 mL*) sweetened coconut

Toast on cookie sheet until light golden (3–5 minutes). Watch carefully to avoid burning.

1 cup (*250 mL*) almond slivers

Toast separately.

⅔ cup (*150 mL*) sweetened condensed milk
1 tsp. (*5 mL*) vanilla
} Combine in a large bowl.

Add toasted coconut and almonds and mix well.

2 egg whites
Pinch of salt
} Beat until stiff but not dry, then fold into the nut mixture.

Drop by tablespoons (*15-mL spoons*) onto cookie sheets lined with greased parchment paper. Bake until just golden at edges (12–14 minutes). Cool and store in airtight container. Makes about 3½ dozen.

*Super sweet, super simple and super delicious.*

# Amaretto Cheesecake

Preheat oven to 350°F (*180°C*).

### Graham Cracker Crust

1⅓ cups (*325 mL*) graham cracker crumbs
⅓ cup (*75 mL*) melted butter
¼ cup (*50 mL*) crushed almonds (untoasted)
¼ cup (*50 mL*) brown sugar

Mix to blend well and press into 9″ (*23 cm*) springform pan.

Bake for 5 minutes. Remove from oven.

2 cups (*500 mL*) soft cream cheese — Cream well.
½ cup (*125 mL*) sour cream — Add and blend.
⅔ cup (*150 mL*) sugar — Add and blend.
3 medium eggs — Beat in one at a time.

1 Tbsp. (*15 mL*) almond extract
1 Tbsp. (*15 mL*) Amaretto liqueur

Add.

Beat mixture until smooth.

Pour over crust. Bake for 30–35 minutes. Let sit for 5 minutes and then put on topping.

### Topping

1 cup (*250 mL*) sour cream
2 Tbsp. (*30 mL*) sugar
2 Tbsp. (*30 mL*) Amaretto liqueur

Mix and smooth gently over cheesecake.

5 Tbsp. (*75 mL*) flaked almonds, toasted

Sprinkle over cheesecake and return to oven for 5 minutes.

Let reach room temperature, then chill for 3–4 hours.

*You may want to rename this cheesecake* Amoretto *and seduce your favourite victim.*

# Toasted Almond Buttercrunch Loaf

| | Preheat oven to 325°F (*160°C*). |
|---|---|
| ½ cup (*125 mL*) butter | Cream until light. |
| ¼ cup (*50 mL*) brown sugar<br>¼ cup (*50 mL*) white sugar<br>½ cup (*125 mL*) flour | Add one at a time, beating well after each addition. |
| ¾ cup (*175 mL*) almonds, toasted and chopped | Stir in.<br><br>Press into bottom and along sides of small loaf pan. |
| ½ cup (*125 mL*) butter<br>¾ cup (*175 mL*) cream cheese } | Using electric mixer, cream together. |
| ⅔ cup (*150 mL*) sugar | Add gradually. |
| 3 eggs | Beat in one at a time. |
| 1¼ cup (*300 mL*) flour<br>½ tsp. (*2 mL*) baking powder } | Sift and stir in. |
| 1 tsp. (*5 mL*) vanilla | Add and mix well. |
| | Pour into crust. |

Bake for 50–60 minutes until golden and knife inserted in centre comes out clean.

*A delicious pound cake coated with candied almonds that can stand on its own — if it survives the prebaking crust-snitchers.*

*Almond*

# Lemon Almond Dacquoise

Preheat oven to 225°F (*54°C*).

## Meringue

Trace three 8″ (*20 cm*) circles on a cookie sheet lined with parchment paper (a standard salad plate can be used as a guide).

1¾ cups (*425 mL*) blanched almonds
½ cup (*125 mL*) sugar

Process together until nuts are finely ground. Set aside.

6 egg whites

Beat until soft peaks form.

1½ cups (*375 mL*) sugar

Add to egg whites very gradually, beating until very stiff peaks form. Fold in almond/sugar mixture.

Use meringue to make three disks on the paper-lined cookie sheet, following circles traced earlier. Bake for 2½ hours or until dry, crisp and lightly coloured. Let cool in oven with door open. Bring to room temperature.

## Lemon Curd Filling

1 cup (*250 mL*) sugar
¾ cup (*175 mL*) freshly squeezed lemon juice
4 whole eggs
4 egg yolks
1½ Tbsp. (*25 mL*) lemon peel, finely grated

Whisk all ingredients in top of double boiler over simmering water until mixture thickens enough to coat back of spoon.

| | |
|---|---|
| 14 Tbsp. (*210 mL*) soft, unsalted butter | Gradually whisk in butter, 1 Tbsp. (*15 mL*) at a time. When completely incorporated, transfer to glass bowl. Cool to room temperature, then chill until cold. |

## To Assemble:

| | |
|---|---|
| 2 cups (*500 mL*) heavy cream | Beat until soft peaks form. |

Put a dollop of lemon curd on platter to keep meringue from slipping. Place one disk of meringue on platter. Spread ⅓ cup (*75 mL*) of lemon curd on top and cover with ⅓ of the whipped cream. Repeat for next layer. Top with third layer of meringue. Spread remaining lemon curd over top and decorate with remaining whipped cream. Dacquoise will be easier to cut if you refrigerate for 6–8 hours before serving.

| | |
|---|---|
| ½ cup (*125 mL*) sliced almonds, toasted<br><br>*or*<br><br>1 lemon, thinly sliced | Use to decorate. |

*A delightful combination of rich lemon custard, crisp and crunchy meringue and smooth, light whipped cream. Perfect in the summer with berries. Amazing as it seems, this dessert can also be served at Passover.*

# Almond Mocha Torte

Preheat oven to 350°F (*180°C*).

### Genoise

| | |
|---|---|
| 8 egg whites | Beat until soft peaks form. |
| ½ cup (*125 mL*) sugar | Gradually add to egg whites and beat until stiff. |
| ½ tsp. (*2 mL*) almond extract<br>1 tsp. (*5 mL*) Amaretto liqueur<br>8 egg yolks, beaten } | Beat well and add to whites. |
| ¾ cup (*175 mL*) blanched<br>almonds, ground<br>½ cup (*125 mL*) flour } | Combine and gently fold into egg mixture, one-quarter at a time. |
| ⅓ cup (*75 mL*) butter, clarified<br>and cooled | Gently fold in. |

Pour into three prepared, round 8″ or 9″ (*20–23 cm*) pans and bake for 20 minutes until the genoise springs back when touched. Cool slightly before filling and frosting with Mocha Cream.

### Mocha Cream

| | |
|---|---|
| 3 oz. (*85 g*) unsweetened<br>chocolate<br>⅓ cup (*75 mL*) strong coffee<br>3 Tbsp. (*45 mL*) instant coffee } | Melt together over low heat, then cool to room temperature. Set aside. |
| 1½ cups (*375 mL*) soft butter | With electric mixer cream until light. |
| 2 cups (*500 mL*) icing sugar | Add gradually. |
| 3 egg yolks | Beat in one at a time. |
| 1 Tbsp. (*15 mL*) coffee liqueur<br>1 tsp. (*5 mL*) vanilla } | Add to egg mixture, then add all to chocolate mixture. Beat until fluffy. |
| | Spread over each layer of genoise, and frost top and sides. |

# Strasbourg Apple Almond Pie

Preheat oven to 375°F (*190°C*).

1 unbaked 9″ (*23 cm*) pie shell

| | |
|---|---|
| 4–5 tart apples, peeled and sliced | Place in bowl. |
| 2 Tbsp. (*30 mL*) sugar<br>1 tsp. (*5 mL*) cinnamon<br>Touch of nutmeg<br>½ cup (*125 mL*) toasted almonds, coarsely chopped | Toss with apples. |

Place in unbaked pie shell and bake for 25 minutes.

| | |
|---|---|
| 4 egg yolks<br>¼ cup (*50 mL*) sugar<br>¼ cup (*50 mL*) light cream<br>¼ cup (*50 mL*) heavy cream | Mix together and pour over apples. |

Return to oven for 25–30 minutes until golden brown and inserted knife comes out clean.

*Apple pie 1990s style!*

# Almond Crunch Crust

| | |
|---|---|
| 1 cup (*250 mL*) toasted almonds<br>¾ cup (*175 mL*) flour<br>¼ cup (*50 mL*) sugar<br>¼ tsp. (*1 mL*) nutmeg | Combine in food processor until nuts are finely chopped. |
| ¼ cup (*50 mL*) cold butter | Add. "Pulse" to combine. |
| 1 egg<br>¼ tsp. (*1 mL*) almond extract | Add and process until mixture forms a ball (10–15 seconds). |
| | Press dough into 10″–11″ (*25–28 cm*) tarte pan. Freeze for 30 minutes. |
| | Preheat oven to 400°F (*200°C*). |
| | Cover dough in pan with foil or parchment paper, then fill pan with pie weights (or dried beans). Bake for 20 minutes. Remove foil and weights and bake another 5 minutes or until golden. |

*This is an easy crust recipe, and one that will work with just about every open tarte. Try it with chocolate as well as fruit tartes. For a Passover tarte, substitute matzo cake meal for flour.*

# Ss and Ds

Batter should be prepared the day before.

1 cup (*250 mL*) soft butter — Cream well.

1 cup (*250 mL*) sugar — Add a little at a time, continuing to cream.

4 eggs — Add one at a time and beat well.

1 tsp (*5 mL*) vanilla — Add.

3½ cups (*875 mL*) flour
1 Tbsp. (*15 mL*) baking powder
2 tsp. (*10 mL*) cinnamon
1 cup (*250 mL*) ground almonds
— Sift together and add with almonds to batter.

Refrigerate overnight.
Preheat oven to 350°F (*180°C*).

2 cups (*500 mL*) ground almonds
2 cups (*500 mL*) sugar
4 tsp. (*20 mL*) cinnamon
— Mix together.

Pinch off a little piece of batter at a time. Roll in nut mixture, working nuts into batter. Form into letters or shapes and place on buttered cookie sheet. Bake for 15–20 minutes until golden. But watch carefully — they can quickly get too dark. Fills six cookie sheets.

*Grandma Faye's original Ss and Os.*

# Traditional Mandelbroit

Preheat oven to 350°F (*180°C*).

| | |
|---|---|
| ½ cup (*125 mL*) vegetable shortening<br>½ cup (*125 mL*) oil | Cream shortening and beat in oil until light. |
| 1 cup (*250 mL*) sugar | Add slowly while beating. |
| 3 eggs | Add one at a time and cream until light. |
| Grated peel of 1 orange<br>Juice of ½ orange<br>1 tsp. (*5 mL*) vanilla | Blend in. |
| 3 cups (*750 mL*) flour<br>¼ cup (*50 mL*) almonds, ground<br>½ tsp. (*2 mL*) salt<br>4 tsp. (*20 mL*) baking powder | Sift together and mix with above. |
| 1 cup (*250 mL*) almonds, toasted and chopped | Fold in. |
| | Divide batter into 4 parts. Oil hands and shape into logs 2–3″ (*5–8 cm*) wide. Bake on prepared cookie sheet for 25 minutes. Remove from oven. Cool 5 minutes, then slice on diagonal. Lay pieces cut side up on cookie sheet. |
| ¼ cup (*50 mL*) cinnamon<br>½ cup (*125 mL*) sugar | Combine. Sprinkle ½ mixture over pieces on cookie sheet. Bake for 8–10 minutes. |

Remove from oven. Turn pieces over and sprinkle with remaining cinnamon and sugar. Bake for 8–10 minutes. Makes about 4 dozen.

*We call this a Jewish Biscotti. Western Canadians call it Komish, and we have no idea why—let us know if you do.*

# Jeanette's Mandelbroit

Preheat oven to 350°F (*180°C*).

| | |
|---|---|
| 1 cup (*250 mL*) sugar<br>1 cup (*250 mL*) oil | Combine and mix on high speed until fluffy. |
| 3 eggs | Add and beat until very fluffy. |
| 1 tsp. (*5 mL*) vanilla<br>¾ tsp. (*4 mL*) almond extract | Blend in. |
| 3 cups (*750 mL*) flour<br>2 tsp. (*10 mL*) baking powder | Combine, then beat in on low speed. |
| 1 cup (*250 mL*) almonds, toasted and coarsely chopped<br>4 handfuls cornflakes, crushed | Stir into mixture by hand. |
| | Divide batter into 3 parts. (This is a sticky dough—don't worry!) Oil hands and shape batter into logs 2–3″ (*5–8 cm*) wide. Bake on prepared cookie sheet for 20 minutes. Remove from oven. Cool 5 minutes, then slice on diagonal. Lay pieces cut side up on cookie sheet. |
| ¼ cup (*50 mL*) cinnamon | Sprinkle ½ of cinnamon over pieces on cookie sheet. Bake for 10 minutes. |
| | Remove from oven. Turn pieces over and sprinkle with remaining cinnamon. Bake for 10 minutes. |
| | Makes about 4 dozen. |

*The cornflakes add a terrific crunch—why not have these for breakfast?!*

# Mocha Almond Truffles

3 Tbsp. (*45 mL*) heavy cream
2 Tbsp. (*30 mL*) unsalted butter

Melt butter with cream in double boiler over hot water on medium heat.

6 oz. (*170 g*) semi-sweet chocolate, finely chopped

Add and stir to melt.

1½ Tbsp. (*25 mL*) coffee, very finely ground
1½ Tbsp. (*25 mL*) Kahlua liqueur

Add and mix in. Chill.

Line baking sheet with waxed paper. Dust with cocoa. Spoon mixture onto sheet in 1-tsp. (*5-mL*) mounds and roll into balls.

3 doz. toasted almonds

Insert an almond into each truffle, then reroll to shape.

Freeze until stiff, then reroll to round shape if necessary. Store in freezer for future use if desired.

Before Serving:

Dip frozen truffles individually in melted chocolate or roll in cocoa.

1–2 oz. (*30–60 g*) semi-sweet chocolate

Melt.

3 doz. toasted almonds

Dip halfway into chocolate. Use one to top each truffle so that your guests will know what's inside.

Serve cool or at room temperature.

*Nobody knows the truffles we've seen—and eaten!*

# Almond Glazed Tarte

Preheat oven to 350°F (*180°C*).

| | |
|---|---|
| 2 cups (*500 mL*) flour<br>½ cup (*125 mL*) sugar<br>½ cup (*125 mL*) butter | Process in food processor until coarse (or blend using pastry blender). |
| 2 eggs<br>½ tsp. (*2 mL*) vanilla<br>½ tsp. (*2 mL*) lemon juice | Beat together, then add to processor and continue to mix until ball forms (or mix until well blended). |
| | Press into 11″ (*28 cm*) ring flan pan. Prick all over with fork. Set aside. |
| ½ cup (*125 mL*) butter<br>⅔ cup (*150 mL*) sugar | Melt butter.<br>Add sugar. |
| 3 eggs, beaten<br>1⅓ cups (*325 mL*) blanched almonds, ground<br>1 Tbsp. (*15 mL*) Amaretto liqueur | Add eggs, then nuts and liqueur. |
| | Pour mixture carefully over crust. |
| 1 cup (*250 mL*) flaked almonds | Gently sprinkle over top so that entire surface is covered. Bake for 35 minutes. |
| ½ cup (*125 mL*) apricot jam<br>2 Tbsp. (*30 mL*) water | Heat and gently brush over tarte while still warm. |

*For those who enjoy a European marzipan-like dessert. Makes a lovely presentation for the afternoon tea table.*

# The Lazy Gourmet Lemon Squares

Preheat oven to 350°F (*180°C*).

## Almond Crust

1 cup (*250 mL*) butter
⅓ cup (*75 mL*) sugar
1¾ cups (*425 mL*) flour
½ cup (*125 mL*) almonds, crushed

} Combine until crumbly and press into bottom of 9″ × 13″ (*23 cm × 33 cm*) pan.

Bake for 20 minutes until light brown.

## Lemon Filling

4 eggs
⅓ cup (*75 mL*) lemon juice
1¼ cups (*300 mL*) sugar

} Mix together well.

⅓ cup (*75 mL*) flour
1 tsp. (*5 mL*) baking powder

} Sift together, add to filling and mix well.

Gently spread mixture over crust and bake for 25 minutes. Cool before cutting. Be careful not to overbake.

# Cinnamon Almond Shortbread

Preheat oven to 350°F (*180°C*).

| | |
|---|---|
| 1 cup (*250 mL*) sugar<br>1 cup (*250 mL*) butter } | Cream well. |
| 1 Tbsp. (*15 mL*) cinnamon<br>1 tsp. (*5 mL*) vanilla<br>1 cup (*250 mL*) almonds,<br>ground } | Mix and add. |
| 1 egg yolk | Add and mix. |
| 2 cups (*500 mL*) flour | Add and mix well. |
| | Press onto a cookie sheet. |
| 1 Tbsp. (*15 mL*) icing sugar | Sprinkle on shortbread. |
| 1 egg white | Whisk, then spread over shortbread with pastry brush. |
| 1 cup (*250 mL*) almonds,<br>ground | Sprinkle over shortbread. |
| 1 Tbsp. (*15 mL*) cinnamon | Sprinkle cinnamon on top. |

Bake for 25 minutes. Cut into squares and separate. Return to warm oven for 25–30 minutes to dry out.

*Deborah's downfall!*

# Almond

## Chocolate Biscotti

| | Preheat oven to 375°F (*190°C*). |
|---|---|
| 1¼ cups (*300 mL*) whole unblanched almonds | Toast and set aside. |

| | |
|---|---|
| 3 eggs<br>½ cup (*125 mL*) packed brown sugar | } Beat together until light. |

| | |
|---|---|
| 2 cups (*500 mL*) flour<br>1½ tsp. (*7 mL*) baking powder<br>¼ tsp. (*1 mL*) salt<br>1 tsp. (*5 mL*) ground anise<br>¼ tsp. (*5 mL*) white pepper<br>1 tsp. (*5 mL*) ground ginger<br>6 Tbsp. (*90 mL*) cocoa powder<br>2 Tbsp. (*30 mL*) instant coffee<br>½ cup (*125 mL*) sugar | } Sift together. Set aside. |

| | |
|---|---|
| 4 oz. (*115 g*) semi-sweet chocolate, chopped | Place in food processor. Add ⅓ cup (*75 mL*) of dry mixture and process until powdery. Add this mixture and the egg mixture to rest of dry ingredients and mix. Add nuts. |

Oil hands and shape dough into 3 long logs. Bake on prepared cookie sheet for 50 minutes. Remove from oven. Cool for 2 minutes. Slice logs into ½ inch (*1 cm*) pieces on the diagonal. Place cookies cut side up on cookie sheet. Reduce oven to 275°F (*135°C*). Return cookies to oven for 20 minutes. Turn cookies over and bake an additional 20 minutes. Makes 3 dozen.

*An authentic Italian biscotti with no oil, butter or fat! What a treat.*

# Chocolate Florentines

Preheat oven to 325°F (*160°C*).

| | |
|---|---|
| ½ cup (*125 mL*) butter<br>¼ cup (*50 mL*) honey<br>¼ cup (*50 mL*) light corn syrup | Place in saucepan and bring to a boil; remove from heat and let cool. |
| 1 cup (*250 mL*) flour<br>1 cup (*250 mL*) almonds, finely chopped<br>2 tsp. (*10 mL*) brandy<br>½ tsp. (*2 mL*) ground ginger | Add and mix well. |

Drop by ½ tsp. (*2 mL*) at least 3″ (*8 cm*) apart onto nonstick or greased cookie sheets. Bake for 12–15 minutes. After about one minute, transfer carefully to cooling rack and let cool completely.

| | |
|---|---|
| 3 oz. (*85 g*) semi-sweet chocolate, melted and slightly cooled | Spread a thin layer of chocolate on a cookie and sandwich with another. |

When all are sandwiched, chill until set, then store in airtight containers in a cool, dry place. Makes about 2 dozen.

*Also known as French lace cookies and usually found only in expensive patisseries.*

# Chocolate Almond Butterscotch Crunch

Preheat oven to 350°F (*180°C*).

| | |
|---|---|
| 1 cup (*250 mL*) sugar<br>1 cup (*250 mL*) brown sugar<br>¾ lb. (1½ cups/*375 mL*) butter, cold<br>2 egg yolks<br>½ tsp. (*2 mL*) vanilla | Mix together. |
| 2 cups (*500 mL*) flour<br>Pinch of salt | Add to above. |
| | Using heel of hand (or rolling pin), flatten mixture into prepared 12″ × 17″ (*30 × 43 cm*) jelly-roll pan. Bake for 45 minutes in centre of oven. |
| 10 oz. (*300 g*) milk chocolate | Melt chocolate and spread on warm baked dough. |
| 1 cup (*250 mL*) almonds, flaked and toasted | Sprinkle nuts over top. |
| | Cut into 2″ (*5 cm*) squares while still warm. |

*A mouth-watering cross between a cookie and a toffee candy.*

# WALNUTS

## Butterscotch Walnut Tarte

Preheat oven to 400°F (*200°C*).

| | |
|---|---|
| 1 lightly baked (pale golden) 9″ (*23 cm*) tarte shell | |
| ⅜ cup (6 Tbsp./*90 mL*) soft butter | Beat well. |
| ⅔ cup (*150 mL*) brown sugar | Add gradually to butter and beat well to dissolve—about 2–3 minutes. |
| ¼ cup (*50 mL*) flour | Beat into mixture. |
| ⅓ cup (*75 mL*) heavy cream 1 tsp. (*5 mL*) vanilla } | Beat in. |
| 1 cup (*250 mL*) walnuts, toasted and coarsely chopped | Stir in. |

Smooth into tarte shell. Bake for 12–15 minutes until just set. Cool.

*As easy as pie—maybe this is where the expression came from!*

# Oatmeal Cookies

| | Preheat oven to 350°F (*180°C*). |
|---|---|
| ¾ cup (*175 mL*) butter | Cream in medium-sized bowl. |
| ¼ cup (*50 mL*) sugar<br>1 cup (*250 mL*) brown sugar | Add and cream until fluffy. |
| 1 egg | Add and beat well. |
| 2 Tbsp. (*30 mL*) orange juice<br>(or water)<br>1 tsp. (*5 mL*) vanilla | Add and mix in thoroughly. |
| 3 cups (*750 mL*) quick oats | Stir in. |
| ⅔ cup (*150 mL*) flour<br>1 tsp. (*5 mL*) cinnamon<br>½ tsp. (*2 mL*) baking soda<br>Pinch of salt | Combine in separate bowl, then add to above and mix well. |
| Optional: | |
| ½ cup (*125 mL*) raisins<br>½ cup (*125 mL*) nuts<br>½ cup (*125 mL*) chocolate<br>chips | Add any or all to dough. |

Bake on prepared cookie sheets for 10–12 minutes, or until edges are golden and centres soft. Makes approximately 3 dozen.

*Full of wholesome fibre and flavour, these cookies make a perfect family snack.*

# Biscotti

| | |
|---|---|
| ¾ cup (*175 mL*) walnuts (or almonds or hazelnuts) | Toast 7–8 minutes at 350°F (*180°C*). Let cool and chop until coarse. |
| | Reduce oven heat to 325°F (*160°C*). |
| ½ cup (*125 mL*) unsalted butter (softened) | Cream until fluffy. |
| ¾ cup (*175 mL*) sugar | Add and beat until light. |
| 2 eggs | Beat in one at a time until fluffy. |
| 1 tsp. (*5 mL*) vanilla<br>1 Tbsp. (*15 mL*) Amaretto liqueur | Blend in. |
| 2 cups + 2 Tbsp. (*530 mL*) flour<br>1½ tsp. (*7 mL*) baking powder<br>¼ tsp. (*1 mL*) salt | Stir into above mixture until just combined. |
| | On lightly floured board, shape dough into 2 logs 12″ (*30 cm*) long × 2″ (*5 cm*) wide. Place on baking sheet and bake for 25 minutes. |
| | Let cool 5 minutes. Then cut ½″ (*1 cm*) slices on the diagonal. Place slices flat on baking sheet. Return to oven and bake 8–10 minutes more until golden. Makes about 3 dozen. |

*We tried the walnut, almond and hazelnut varieties of this Biscotti, and the jury is still out on which one wins first prize. Try them all yourself.*

# Grandma's Sour Cream Coffee Cake

Preheat oven to 350°F (*180°C*).

| | |
|---|---|
| 1 cup (*250 mL*) soft butter | Cream well. |
| 1 cup (*250 mL*) sugar | Add gradually. |
| 3 eggs | Add eggs, one at a time, mixing well after each addition. |

1 cup (*250 mL*) sour cream
1 tsp. (*5 mL*) lemon extract
} Add to above.

3 cups (*750 mL*) flour
3 tsp. (*15 mL*) baking powder
½ tsp. (*2 mL*) baking soda
} Sift well and add.

Place half the batter in 9″ (*23 cm*) prepared springform pan.

## Centre and Topping

1 cup (*250 mL*) brown sugar
3 Tbsp. (*45 mL*) cinnamon
¾ cup (*175 mL*) walnuts, chopped
¾ cup (*175 mL*) chocolate chips
*or* 4 oz. (*115 g*) semi-sweet chocolate, grated
} Mix all ingredients together. Sprinkle cake with half the chocolate nut mixture. Cover with rest of batter. Sprinkle with remainder of mixture.

Bake for 50–60 minutes until done.

# Lynnie's Baklava

Preheat oven to 350°F (*180°C*).

1½ cups (*375 mL*) walnuts, ground
2 tsp. (*10 mL*) cinnamon
2 Tbsp. (*30 mL*) icing sugar

Mix together.

1 cup (*250 mL*) butter

Melt butter.

½ lb. (*250 g*) filo

Layer filo in 9″ × 13″ (*23 cm × 33 cm*) baking pan (preferably stainless steel or glass), brushing every sheet with melted butter. Sprinkle nut mixture on every third sheet.

With a sharp knife, score into squares or diamond shapes and bake for 30 minutes.

## Syrup

½ cup (*125 mL*) honey
¾ cup (*175 mL*) water
1¼ cups (*300 mL*) sugar
Juice of ½ lemon
1 cinnamon stick

Mix together and bring to boil. Boil for 10 minutes, then simmer 10 minutes longer.

Cool, then pour over filo. Let sit 2–3 hours or overnight. DO NOT REFRIGERATE. Cut completely through to serve.

*Can you believe how easy this is?!*

# Our High-Priced Gourmet Cookies

Preheat oven to 350°F (*180°C*).

| | |
|---|---|
| 2¼ cups (*550 mL*) flour<br>1 cup (*250 mL*) sugar<br>¼ tsp. (*1 mL*) baking soda | Sift together and set aside. |
| ½ lb. (*250 g*) butter at room temperature<br>1 cup (*250 mL*) brown sugar | Cream together until light and fluffy. Scrape sides of bowl to ensure that all butter is thoroughly creamed. |
| 2 eggs | Beat one at a time into butter/sugar mix until just combined. |
| | Add flour mixture all at once and mix until just incorporated. |
| 2 cups (*500 mL*) semi-sweet chocolate chunks<br>1 cup (*250 mL*) walnuts or pecans | Add to dough with hands or a heavy wooden spoon. |

Scoop dough onto prepared cookie sheet, making each cookie a 1-Tbsp. (*15 mL*) scoop. Bake for 10 minutes until crusty outside and gooey inside. Do not overbake. Makes 2–3 dozen cookies.

*We think these are much better than those high-priced cookies in the mall. For an incredible experience, bite into the cookie while the chocolate is still warm and melted.*

# *New* New York Blondies

|  |  |
|---|---|
|  | Preheat oven to 325°F (*160°C*). |
| ½ cup (*125 mL*) butter | Melt. Place in bowl. |
| 1¼ cups (*300 mL*) brown sugar | Add to melted butter. |
| ½ tsp. (*2 mL*) vanilla | Add. |
| 1 egg, whisked | Add to mixture. |
| 1 cup (*250 mL*) flour 1¼ tsp. (*6 mL*) baking powder } | Combine and add to above. |
| ½ cup (*125 mL*) chocolate chips ½ cup (*125 mL*) walnuts, chopped } | Stir in. |
|  | Spread dough into prepared 8″ (*20 cm*) square pan. Bake for approximately 30 minutes. |

*The batter for these is spreadable rather than pourable. The result is a chewier and fudgier square than our original Blondies.*

## Maple Walnut Torte

Preheat oven to 350°F (*180°C*).

4 cups (*1 L*) walnuts
1 Tbsp. (*15 mL*) sugar

} "Pulse" together in food processor until nuts are finely ground.

6 egg yolks
⅔ cup (*150 mL*) sugar
1½ Tbsp. (*25 mL*) maple syrup

} Beat in small bowl until mixture triples in volume (approximately 5 minutes). It should be very thick and light. Set aside.

6 egg whites — Beat in large bowl until soft peaks form.

1 Tbsp. (*15 mL*) sugar — Add to egg whites. Beat to stiff peaks.

Fold walnuts into yolk mixture. Fold in ½ the whites to lighten the texture, then fold in the rest.

Pour into 9″ (*23 cm*) springform pan buttered and lined with wax paper round. Bake for 50–60 minutes. Cool *thoroughly* before icing with Maple Buttercream.

*We especially recommend this nutty torte to people who are looking for recipes without flour.*

## Maple Buttercream

1 tsp. (*5 mL*) instant espresso powder
2 tsp. (*10 mL*) water
½ cup (*125 mL*) maple syrup

} Combine in heavy saucepan and bring to boil over low heat. Cook 10 minutes. Remove from heat and let cool to room temperature.

1 cup (*500 mL*) unsalted butter, softened — In bowl, beat until very pale and fluffy.

¾ cup (*175 mL*) icing sugar — Gradually add to butter and beat until creamy.

Gradually beat in cooled syrup. Reserve 1 Tbsp. (*15 mL*) butter-cream for decoration if desired. Frost cooled cake.

½–¾ cup (*125–175 mL*) walnut pieces, lightly toasted and chopped

Press nuts into sides, around the bottom of the cake, as garnish.

Reheat extra maple syrup slightly, then "spritz" it decoratively onto top of cake.

# Very Tart Walnut Pie

Preheat oven to 350°F (*180°C*).

1 9″ (*23 cm*) pie shell, prebaked to golden

¾ cup (*175 mL*) raisins
1½ Tbsp. (*25 mL*) lemon peel, grated
½ cup (*125 mL*) lemon juice

Soak raisins and peel in juice, then set aside.

½ cup (*125 mL*) butter
⅓ cup (*75 mL*) sugar
¼ cup (*50 mL*) brown sugar
1 tsp. (*5 mL*) cinnamon

Cream together until very light and fluffy.

3 eggs

Add to butter/sugar mixture one at a time, beating well after each addition.

Stir in raisin mixture.

⅔ cup (*150 mL*) coarsely chopped walnuts

Stir in nuts. (Mixture will appear a bit curdled.)

Pour into pie shell and bake for 30–40 minutes until set. Cool. Serve with ice cream or whipped cream.

*The lemon does great things to walnuts and sugar. Pucker up for thank yous.*

# Maple Walnut Cheesecake

Preheat oven to 350°F (*180°C*).

## Crust

1⅓ cups (*325 mL*) graham wafer crumbs

Place in bowl.

⅓ cup (*75 mL*) melted butter
3 Tbsp. (*45 mL*) walnuts, ground
3 Tbsp. (*45 mL*) maple syrup

Mix well and add to crumbs.

Press into 9″ (*23 cm*) prepared springform pan. Bake for 5 minutes.

## Centre

2 cups (*500 mL*) soft cream cheese
½ cup (*125 mL*) sour cream
⅓ cup (*75 mL*) sugar
⅓ cup (*75 mL*) maple syrup
1 tsp. (*5 mL*) vanilla
3 eggs

Combine and beat until light. Pour over crust.

Return to oven for 35–40 minutes.

## Topping

1 cup (*250 mL*) sour cream
3 Tbsp. (*45 mL*) maple syrup

Mix and gently spread over cake.

4 Tbsp. (*60 mL*) walnuts, toasted

Sprinkle over cake and return to oven for 5 minutes.

Chill 3–4 hours before serving.

*The lightest of our cheesecakes.*

# Walnut Fudge Flan

Preheat oven to 350°F (*180°C*).

### Shortbread Flan Crust

¾ cup (*175 mL*) butter
1½ cups (*375 mL*) flour
3 Tbsp. (*45 mL*) sugar

Using food processor, process until crumbly.

1½ Tbsp. (*25 mL*) lemon juice

Add juice and process until mixture forms a ball.
*or*
Cut dry ingredients with pastry blender and add juice.

Press into bottom and sides of a ring flan pan and bake for 15 minutes.

1 cup (*250 mL*) sugar
3 eggs
⅓ cup (*75 mL*) melted butter
½ tsp. (*2 mL*) vanilla
3½ cups (*875 mL*) walnuts, crushed

Mix well, pour over crust and bake for 25–30 minutes or more. Chill.

### Glaze

1 cup (*250 mL*) chocolate chips
3 Tbsp. (*45 mL*) butter
1 tsp. (*5 mL*) vanilla

Melt chips.
Add butter and blend.
Add vanilla.
Spread over flan.

*Makes 15 spectacular slices. This flan can do nothing to hide its richness.*

*Walnut*

# Money–Back Guarantee Brownies

|  | Preheat oven to 350°F (*180°C*). |
|---|---|
| 1 cup (*250 mL*) butter | Melt butter. |
| 1 cup (*250 mL*) white sugar<br>1 cup (*250 mL*) brown sugar<br>¾ cup (*175 mL*) cocoa } | Add and blend well. |
| 3 large eggs | Beat in, one at a time. |
| 1 cup (*250 mL*) flour<br>1½ tsp. (*7 mL*) baking powder } | Sift into mixture and stir. |
| 1½ tsp. (*7 mL*) vanilla<br>1 cup (*250 mL*) walnuts,<br>chopped } | Add. |

Incredible Chocolate Icing
(page 10)

Pour into prepared 9″ × 13″ (*23 cm × 33 cm*) pan. Bake for 30 minutes. (Centre will be firm but not hard.) Ice when cool.

*At the Lazy Gourmet we offer a money-back guarantee if these are not the best brownies you've ever tasted!*

# Old New York Blondies

|  | Preheat oven to 350°F (*180°C*). |
|---|---|
| 1 cup (*250 mL*) butter | Melt. |
| 2 cups (*500 mL*) brown sugar | Add and mix well. |
| 4 eggs | Beat in, one at a time. |
| 1½ cups (*375 mL*) flour<br>2 tsp. (*10 mL*) baking powder | Sift and add all at once. |
| 1½ cups (*375 mL*) chocolate chips<br>1 cup (*250 mL*) walnuts, chopped | Mix together and add. |
| 2 tsp. (*10 mL*) vanilla | Add. |
|  | Pour dough into prepared 9″ × 13″ (*22 cm × 33 cm*) pan. |
| ¼ cup (*50 mL*) walnuts<br>¼ cup (*50 mL*) chocolate chips | Mix together and sprinkle over top. |
|  | Bake for 30 minutes. |

*A popular New York treat. When you wish you were in the Big Apple, bake up a batch.*

## Walnut Dream Bars

Preheat oven to 325°F (*160°C*).

½ cup (*125 mL*) butter
3 Tbsp. (*45 mL*) brown sugar
1 cup (*250 mL*) flour

Mix well and press into an 8″ (*20 cm*) square pan.

Bake for 15 minutes.

2 eggs
1 cup (*250 mL*) brown sugar
½ tsp. (*2 mL*) baking powder
2 Tbsp. (*30 mL*) flour
1 tsp. (*5 mL*) vanilla
¾ cup (*175 mL*) walnuts, chopped
½ cup (*125 mL*) long threaded coconut

Mix well and pour over crust.

Bake for 20 minutes longer.
Cool before cutting.

*Sweet and gooey. A perfect antidote for exercise.*


## Oatmeal Chocolate Chip Squares

Preheat oven to 350°F (*180°C*).

1¾ cups (*425 mL*) boiling water
1¾ cups (*425 mL*) oatmeal

Combine and let stand for 10 minutes.

3½ Tbsp. (*55 mL*) butter
1½ cups (*375 mL*) white sugar
1¼ cups (*300 mL*) light brown sugar

Add to above and stir until butter melts.

2 large eggs

Add and mix well.

1¾ cups (*425 mL*) flour
3 Tbsp. (*45 mL*) cocoa    }    Sift and add to above.
1½ tsp. (*7 mL*) baking soda

Let cool.

5 oz. (*140 g*) small chocolate    Add to cooled batter.
chips

2 oz. (*60 g*) chocolate chips

Pour batter into prepared 9″ × 13″ (*23 cm × 33 cm*) pan. Sprinkle top with chips and bake for 40 minutes.

*A delicious lunchbox treat.*

# Walnut Chip Banana Bread

Preheat oven to 350°F (*180°C*).

2 large ripe bananas, mashed
1 cup (*250 mL*) sugar
2 eggs    }    Combine and mix well.
½ cup (*125 mL*) oil

1¼ cups (*300 mL*) flour
1 tsp. (*5 mL*) baking soda    }    Sift and mix in.

½ cup (*125 mL*) walnuts,
chopped    }    Add.
½ cup (*125 mL*) chocolate chips

*or* 2 oz. (*60 g*) semi-sweet
chocolate, chopped fine

Pour into buttered loaf pan. Bake for 1 hour until loaf springs back when touched.

*This bread freezes well and stays fresh when refrigerated. You'll never find a better banana bread recipe!*

# PEANUTS

## Peanut Caramel Pie

Preheat oven to 350°F (*180°C*).

1 unbaked 9″ (*23 cm*) pie shell

¼ cup (*50 mL*) brown sugar
¼ cup (*50 mL*) white sugar
1½ cups (*375 mL*) corn syrup

Combine in saucepan, stir and bring to boil.

Remove from heat.

¼ cup (*50 mL*) butter

Add butter and mix well.

Let sit until slightly cooled.

3 eggs

Beat eggs together, then add to mixture, beating well.

1 cup (*250 mL*) salted peanuts, chopped
1 tsp. (*5 mL*) vanilla

Add and pour into unbaked shell.

Bake for 45 minutes.

*A recession pecan pie.*

# Recipes

## Peanut Butter Crispy Squares

| | |
|---|---|
| ½ cup (*125 mL*) sugar<br>½ cup (*125 mL*) corn syrup | Combine and heat until mixture boils. Remove from heat. |
| ½ cup (*125 mL*) peanut butter<br>½ tsp. (*2 mL*) vanilla | Add and mix well. |
| 3 cups (*750 mL*) rice crisp cereal<br>1 cup (*250 mL*) peanuts,<br>coarsely chopped | Stir into above mixture until everything is coated. |
| ½ cup (*125 mL*) chocolate chips | Add chips last. |
| | Pat into prepared 8″ (*20 cm*) square pan. Cool and cut into bars. |

*Great as a lunchbox snack or when you need to produce treats in a hurry.*

## Peanut Butter Truffles

| | |
|---|---|
| 1 cup (*250 mL*) crunchy peanut butter<br>4 Tbsp. (*60 mL*) soft butter<br>1¼ cups (*300 mL*) icing sugar | Mix well and then form into balls. |
| | Chill well or freeze. |
| 6 oz. (*170 g*) semi-sweet chocolate, melted | Dip peanut butter balls in melted chocolate and set on waxed paper. |
| | Chill before serving. |

# Peanut Butter Nanaimo Bars

### Layer One

½ cup (*125 mL*) butter
¼ cup (*50 mL*) sugar
1 egg
1 tsp. (*5 mL*) vanilla
1 Tbsp. (*15 mL*) cocoa

} Mix together and set over boiling water until *slightly* thickened. Stir occasionally.

2 cups (*500 mL*) graham cracker crumbs
1 cup (*250 mL*) dessicated coconut
½ cup (*125 mL*) peanuts, chopped

} Mix and add to above.

Press into buttered 9″ (*23 cm*) square pan so that base is evenly spread. Chill 15 minutes.

### Layer Two

½ cup (*125 mL*) peanut butter
2 Tbsp. (*30 mL*) soft butter
2 Tbsp. (*30 mL*) custard powder
2 cups (*500 mL*) icing sugar
4 Tbsp. (*60 mL*) milk

} Mix well together and spread over Layer One.

Chill for 15 minutes.

### Layer Three

4–5 oz. (*120–150 g*) semi-sweet chocolate
1 Tbsp. (*15 mL*) butter

} Melt over hot water and spread over Layer Two.

Chill. Score chocolate with sharp paring knife, then cut into squares.

*No sooner had the Lazy Gourmet invented this recipe than several bakeries tried to duplicate it. Here's the real thing.*

# Peanut Brittle

Butter large marble slab or two cookie sheets.

2 cups (*500 mL*) white sugar
1 cup (*250 mL*) brown sugar
1¾ cups (*425 mL*) light corn syrup
1 cup (*250 mL*) water

In heavy saucepan, combine and cook until candy thermometer reads 240°F (*115°C*).

5 cups (*1.25 L*) raw peanuts

Add and cook until thermometer reaches 295°F (*145°C*).

2 Tbsp. (*30 mL*) butter

Remove from heat and add.

2 tsp. (*10 mL*) baking soda
½ tsp. (*2 mL*) salt

Add and beat mixture vigorously.

Pour onto slab or sheets, spreading as thinly as possible. When cool, break up. Makes about 4 dozen pieces.

*If you are feeling experimental, try making this with other nuts or spreading the brittle with melted chocolate.*

# Chocolatized Peanut Butter Pie

1 fully baked 9"–11"
(*23–28 cm*) chocolate crust
shell (use either a chocolate
crumb crust, p. 14, or
Chocolate Crust, p. 33)

## Filling

| | |
|---|---|
| 8 oz. (*250 g*) cream cheese (don't use the commercial whipped variety) 1 cup (*250 mL*) creamy unsalted peanut butter | Beat together until smooth. |
| ¾ cup (*175 mL*) sugar (extra-fine or berry is best) | Beat in to dissolve sugar. |
| 1½ cups (*350 mL*) heavy cream | Beat until soft peaks form. Fold ¼ into peanut butter mixture to lighten texture, then fold in the rest. |

Optional:

| | |
|---|---|
| 3 Tbsp. (*45 mL*) peanut butter 2 Tbsp. (*30 mL*) sugar ¼ cup (*50 mL*) water | Beat together until well blended. Swirl into pie filling. |
| | Mound into cooled pie shell. Chill well—at least 2 hours or until solid. |

## Topping

| | |
|---|---|
| ⅓ cup (*75 mL*) heavy cream | Heat to boiling. |
| ¾ cup (*175 mL*) chocolate chips | Stir in until chocolate is melted. |
| 1 tsp. (*5 mL*) vanilla | Add. |

Cool 10 minutes, then spread over pie.

Chill 30 minutes or until chocolate sets.

*Considered by many who sampled recipes from this book to be one of the best!*

# Peanut Butter Chunk Cookies

Preheat oven to 350°F (*180°C*).

| | |
|---|---|
| ¾ cup (*175 mL*) sugar<br>⅔ cup (*150 mL*) brown sugar<br>½ cup (*125 mL*) butter | Cream together until fluffy. |
| 2 eggs | Add and mix until light. |
| 1 tsp. (*5 mL*) vanilla<br>1¼ cups (*300 mL*) peanut butter | Add. |
| 1 cup (*250 mL*) flour<br>½ tsp. (*2 mL*) baking soda | Combine, then add and mix until just blended—*do not overmix*. |
| ⅓–½ lb. (*200–250 g*) milk chocolate | Chop and add. |

Roll into 1" (*2.5 cm*) balls and press with back of fork onto prepared cookie sheet. Bake for 12–13 minutes. Do not overbake. Makes about 3 dozen.

*Yes, this is the recipe that you've been begging us for!*

# Upscale Peanut Butter Squares

| | |
|---|---|
| ¾ cup (*175 mL*) icing sugar<br>½ cup (*125 mL*) melted butter<br>1½ cups (*375 mL*) chocolate cookie crumbs<br>½ cup (*125 mL*) peanut butter | Mix together and press into 9″ × 13″ (*23 cm × 33 cm*) pan that has been lightly sprayed with no-stick cooking spray. |
| ¾ cup (*175 mL*) icing sugar<br>½ cup (*125 mL*) melted butter<br>1½ cups (*375 mL*) graham wafer crumbs<br>½ cup (*125 mL*) peanut butter | Combine thoroughly. Gently spread over first mixture. Chill well. |
| 10 oz. (*300 g*) semi-sweet chocolate chips<br>⅓ cup (*75 mL*) butter | Melt together. Pour over peanut butter mixture. |

Chill to set.

Try decorating these with swirls or chevrons made with melted peanut butter chips. Refrigerate until firm. Cut into small squares with sharp knife.

*These squares keep well for up to a month in the fridge. But once they are discovered . . . good-bye.*

# TRADITIONAL RECIPES

## Passover Mocha Squares

Preheat oven to 325°F (*160°C*).

4 oz. (*115 g*) unsweetened chocolate
½ lb. (*250 g*) butter

Melt and set aside.

4 eggs
2 cups (*500 mL*) sugar
1 tsp. (*5 mL*) salt

Beat together, then add to cooled chocolate mixture.

2 tsp. (*10 mL*) instant coffee
1 cup (*250 mL*) matzo cake meal

Add and mix.

Place in prepared 9″ × 13″ (*23 cm × 34 cm*) pan.

1 cup (*250 mL*) walnuts, chopped

Sprinkle over batter.

Bake for 30 minutes.

*With recipes like this, who needs flour? This is the best brownie recipe we have found. Be sure not to overbake.*

# Miriam's Passover Komish or Mandelbroit

Preheat oven to 350°F (*180°C*).

| | |
|---|---|
| 3 eggs<br>5 Tbsp. (*75 mL*) oil<br>¾ cup (*175 mL*) sugar<br>Peel of one lemon, grated<br>Peel of one orange, grated | Beat together. |
| 1¼ cup (*300 mL*) matzo cake meal<br>½ cup (*125 mL*) almonds, toasted<br>¼ cup (*50 mL*) coconut | Combine and stir in. |

Refrigerate for 10 minutes.

Remove from fridge. Divide batter into 3 parts. Oil hands and shape dough into logs 2–3" (*5–8 cm*) wide. Bake on prepared cookie sheet for 20 minutes. Remove from oven. Cool, then slice on diagonal. Lay pieces cut side up on cookie sheet.

| | |
|---|---|
| 2 Tbsp. (*30 mL*) cinnamon<br>⅓ cup (*75 mL*) sugar | Combine. Sprinkle ½ mixture over pieces on cookie sheet. Bake for 4 minutes. |

Remove from oven. Turn pieces over and sprinkle with remaining cinnamon and sugar. Bake for 4 minutes.

Makes about 4 dozen.

*Called Komish in western Canada, these Mandelbroit are just as good, but not as light, as our other Mandelbroit recipes.*

# Chocolate Orange Passover Cake

|  |  |
|---|---|
|  | Preheat oven to 350°F (*180°C*). |
| 9 egg whites | Beat until foamy. |
| ½ cup (*125 mL*) sugar | Slowly add to egg whites, beating until stiff. |
| 9 egg yolks<br>½ cup (*125 mL*) sugar | Beat together, then fold into whites. |
| 1 cup (*250 mL*) ground almonds<br>½ cup (*125 mL*) chopped almonds (or walnuts)<br>1 Tbsp. (*15 mL*) potato starch<br>3 Tbsp. (*45 mL*) sifted matzo cake meal<br>1 Tbsp. (*15 mL*) powdered instant coffee<br>4 oz. (*115 g*) semi-sweet chocolate, coarsely grated<br>Grated peel of 1 large orange | Combine, then gently fold into egg mixture. |

Pour batter into a 9 or 10″ (*23–26 cm*) tube pan lightly greased with oil and floured with matzo cake meal. Bake for 45 minutes. When cool, cover with Chocolate Honey Glaze.

# Chocolate Honey Glaze

|  |  |
|---|---|
| 6 oz. (*170 g*) semi-sweet chocolate, chopped<br>4 oz. (*115 g*) unsalted butter<br>2–3 Tbsp. (*30–45 mL*) honey | Melt together, stirring until smooth. |

Pour over cooled cake. Makes 1 cup (*250 mL*).

*Without the glaze, this rich, nutty combination of orange and chocolate makes an exceptional breakfast cake.*

# Almond Lemon Meringues

Preheat oven to 275°F (*140°C*).

| | |
|---|---|
| 1 cup (*250 mL*) minus 2 Tbsp. (*30 mL*) sliced blanched almonds<br>2 Tbsp. (*30 mL*) sugar | Process together in food processor until nuts are finely ground. Set aside. |
| 3 egg whites | Beat until soft peaks form. |
| ½ cup (*125 mL*) sugar | Add gradually to egg whites. Beat until stiff peaks form. |
| ¼ tsp. (*1 mL*) almond extract<br>⅛ tsp. (*0.5 mL*) lemon extract (optional) | Beat into egg-white mixture. |
| | Fold in ground almonds. |
| Finely grated peel of 1 lemon | Fold in. |
| | Drop batter from teaspoon (*5-mL spoon*) onto parchment-lined (or buttered and floured) cookie sheets 1″ (*2.5 cm*) apart. Press 1 sliced almond onto top of each cookie. |

Place cookies in oven and immediately reduce heat to 200°F (*100°C*). Bake 1½ hours. Cool on cookie sheets. Store in airtight tins. Will keep for up to 1 month.

Makes 2–3 dozen.

*Another delicious addition to our Passover repertoire—but great for serving during the rest of the year, too.*

# Chocolate Coconut Macaroons

Preheat oven to 375°F (*190°C*).

| | |
|---|---|
| 4 oz. (*115 g*) semi-sweet chocolate<br>2 oz. (*60 g*) unsweetened chocolate | Melt together. Set aside and cool until tepid. |
| 2 egg whites | Beat 1 minute until soft peaks form. |
| ½ cup (*125 mL*) sugar | Add to egg whites, 1 Tbsp. (*15 mL*) at a time, beating after each addition until mixture is stiff (approximately 1 minute). |
| 1 tsp. (*5 mL*) vanilla<br>1 tsp. (*5 mL*) instant espresso coffee | Dissolve coffee in vanilla, then add to egg-white mixture. |
| | Fold in melted chocolate. |
| 2 cups (*500 mL*) shredded coconut<br>½ cup (*125 mL*) toasted almond slivers (optional) | Fold in. |

Drop by large tablespoons (*15-mL spoons*) onto cookie sheet lined with parchment paper. Bake for 12–13 minutes or until just crusty. Cool, then remove to rack. Makes about 2 dozen large macaroons.

*Our children David and Mira snuck off into a corner with a tin of these cookies when they were first invented. Now their favourite word is "macaroons."*

# Passover Schmoo Torte

Preheat oven to 350°F (*180°C*).

## Torte

12 egg yolks
¾ cup (*175 mL*) sugar
1½ Tbsp. (*22 mL*) lemon juice
} Beat together until light.

2 cups (*500 mL*) pecans, finely ground
⅓ cup (*75 mL*) matzo cake meal
} Mix together and add to egg mixture.

12 egg whites — Beat until soft peaks form.

Pinch of salt
1 cup (*250 mL*) sugar
} Slowly add, beating to stiff peaks, then fold into yolk mixture.

Place in ungreased tube pan. Bake 55–60 minutes. Invert to cool before removing from pan.

## Filling

2 cups (*500 mL*) heavy cream
3 Tbsp. (*45 mL*) icing sugar (optional)
1 tsp. (*5 mL*) vanilla
} Beat together until soft peaks form.

Slice cake into 5 layers. Spread each layer with whipped cream filling, leaving enough to cover top and sides of cake.

## Caramel Sauce

1 cup (*250 mL*) brown sugar
1 cup (*250 mL*) heavy cream
¼ cup (*50 mL*) unsalted butter
} Mix together and bring to a boil for 6–7 minutes. Remove from heat.

Refrigerate until 10 minutes before ready to serve. Drizzle room-temperature sauce over cake and serve the rest on the side.

*Thank goodness this favourite torte can be adapted to a Passover table. Now it can be eaten every night of the year except Yom Kippur!*

# Apple Pecan Kugel

Preheat oven to 350°F (*180°C*).

5 Tbsp. (*75 mL*) melted butter
1 cup (*250 mL*) brown sugar
1 cup (*250 mL*) pecan halves

Mix and press into bottom of tube pan.

1 lb. (*500 g*) fresh fettucine
*or* 12 oz. (*340 g*) dried fettucine
(flat egg noodles)

Cook fresh fettucine for 5 minutes in boiling water (about 9 minutes for dried fettucine). Drain and rinse with cold water. Set aside.

¾ cup (*175 mL*) sugar
5 eggs
1 cup (*250 mL*) sour cream
1 tsp. (*5 mL*) vanilla

Mix well together and set aside.

2 cups (*500 mL*) apples, peeled and chopped
1 Tbsp. (*15 mL*) cinnamon
¼ cup (*50 mL*) flour

Combine.

Now mix noodles, apples and egg mixture. Pour into tube pan. Bake for one hour. Let sit for 15 minutes. Invert and serve warm or at room temperature.

*Rosh Hashana, the Jewish New Year, is always welcomed by eating sweet apples. What could be more inviting than this fabulous kugel?*

# Rugelah, Rogelach or Kuffels

| | |
|---|---|
| 2 cups (*500 mL*) flour<br>½ lb. (*250 g*) butter | Pulse on and off in food processor. |
| 1 cup (*250 mL*) cream cheese | Add to flour and butter and mix. |
| | Divide into 4 balls and flatten into disks. Wrap and refrigerate for 1 hour. |
| ½ cup (*125 mL*) brown sugar<br>2 Tbsp. (*30 mL*) cinnamon<br>3 Tbsp. (*45 mL*) cocoa | Mix together. |
| ¼ cup (*50 mL*) unsalted butter | Melt and set aside. |
| | Preheat oven to 350°F (*180°C*). |
| | Roll out dough as you would a pie crust, one disk at a time, into 6″ (*15 cm*) circles. Brush with melted butter. Sprinkle with cinnamon-sugar mixture. Cut each disk pizza-style into 8 wedges. Roll up pastry wedges, starting with the base of the triangle, and curve to form crescents. |
| 1 egg<br>2 Tbsp. (*30 mL*) milk | Mix together, then brush over pastry. |

Bake on prepared cookie sheets for 20–25 minutes until golden. Makes about 40.

*The mystery is solved. Now you know that rugelah, rogelach and kuffels are all names for the tiny, rich and flavourful crescents that have enjoyed enormous popularity, especially in New York City, for years. Chances are they're the first to go at bar mitzvah luncheons.*

# Winnipeg Bar Mitzvah Torte

Preheat oven to 350°F (*180°C*).

| | |
|---|---|
| 1 egg<br>1 cup (*250 mL*) sugar | Beat together. |
| 1 cup (*250 mL*) butter, melted<br>and slightly cooled | Add. |
| 2½ cups (*625 mL*) flour<br>⅛ tsp. (*0.5 mL*) baking soda | Sift together. |
| | Mix all together.<br>Knead slightly. |

Divide into four prepared round 8″ or 9″ (*20–23 cm*) pans and bake for 15–18 minutes, until golden brown. Cool slightly before removing from pans.

## Chocolate Filling

| | |
|---|---|
| 3 egg yolks<br>¾ cup (*175 mL*) sugar | Mix together in saucepan. |
| ¼ cup (*50 mL*) cocoa<br>2¼ cups (*550 mL*) milk | Add cocoa and milk and bring to a boil. |
| ¼ cup (*50 mL*) cornstarch<br>dissolved in ¾ cup<br>(*175 mL*) milk | Add and whisk until smooth and thick. |
| 1½ Tbsp. (*25 mL*) butter<br>1 tsp. (*5 mL*) vanilla | Add and let cool. Stir frequently. |

When cake and custard are cool, spread filling between layers and over top. *Chill for at least 24 hours.*

*A bar mitzvah sweet-table standard delight. Always the first to go.*

# Traditional

## Hamantaschen

### Fillings

#### Caramel Pecan Filling

| | |
|---|---|
| ¾ cup (*175 mL*) sugar<br>¼ cup (*50 mL*) water | In a medium saucepan, bring to a boil. |
| 1¾ cup (*425 mL*) chopped pecans, toasted<br>½ cup (*125 mL*) unsalted butter<br>½ cup (*125 mL*) warm milk | Add to sugar/water mixture. Turn down heat. Simmer until thick, approximately 10 minutes. Remove from heat. |
| ¼ cup (*50 mL*) honey | Add to mixture. |
| | Refrigerate until set, then use to fill hamantaschen. |

#### Chocolate Filling

| | |
|---|---|
| ½ cup (*125 mL*) cocoa<br>½ cup (*125 mL*) sugar<br>¼ cup (*50 mL*) heavy cream<br>1 cup (*250 mL*) chopped walnuts, toasted<br>½ cup (*125 mL*) chocolate chips | Combine in a bowl. Use to fill hamantaschen. |

#### Poppyseed Almond Filling

| | |
|---|---|
| ½ cup (*125 mL*) sugar<br>2 tsp. (*10 mL*) honey<br>¼ cup (*50 mL*) water | Combine in medium saucepan and heat on medium just until sugar melts, stirring constantly. |
| 1 cup (*250 mL*) poppyseeds<br>1 Tbsp. (*15 mL*) lemon peel, finely grated<br>⅓ cup (*75 mL*) raisins<br>1 tsp. (*5 mL*) brandy | Add to sugar mixture and cook on low heat for 15 minutes, until gooey. Remove from heat. Allow to cool. |

# Recipes

| | |
|---|---|
| ½ cup (*125 mL*) almonds, toasted and chopped | Add to cooled poppyseed mixture. |
| | Use to fill hamantaschen. |

## Dough

| | |
|---|---|
| ½ cup (*125 mL*) butter<br>½ cup (*125 mL*) sugar | Beat together until fluffy. |
| 2 eggs | Beat in. |
| Grated peel and juice of one orange<br>2 cups (*500 mL*) flour<br>1½ tsp. (*7 mL*) baking powder<br>¼ tsp. (*1 mL*) salt | Combine. Add to above and mix until a dough is formed. |

Divide dough into three portions. Roll out each portion until it is ¼" (*0.5 cm*) thick. Cut into 2½" (*6 cm*) rounds (an upside-down cup works well) and fill.

## To Assemble:

Preheat oven to 350°F (*180°C*).

Place 1 tsp. (*5 mL*) of filling of your choice in centre of round. Fold edges of round from three sides towards centre to form a triangle, leaving a bit of the filling visible. Pinch to secure. Repeat until all hamantaschen are filled. Place on prepared cookie sheets ½" (*1 cm*) apart.

| | |
|---|---|
| 1 egg | Beat. Brush over pastries. |
| | Bake for 10 minutes, until golden. |

*This specialty cookie is made each year during the festival of Purim. These different fillings give lots of variety to a delicious treat.*

# Lazy Gourmet Christmas Cake

Preheat oven to 325°F (*160°C*).

|  |  |
|---|---|
| 4 cups (*1 L*) pitted whole dates<br>4 cups (*1 L*) walnut halves<br>½ cup (*125 mL*) dried apricots, chopped | Combine in large bowl. |
| ¼ cup (*50 mL*) flour | Sprinkle over fruit and nuts and toss to coat well. Set aside. |
| 3 egg yolks<br>⅓ cup (*75 mL*) sugar<br>⅓ cup (*75 mL*) brown sugar | Combine in large bowl. Beat until light and fluffy. |
| 3 Tbsp. (*45 mL*) unsalted butter, melted and cooled<br>3 Tbsp. (*45 mL*) heavy cream<br>1 Tbsp. (*15 mL*) brandy<br>1 tsp. (*5 mL*) orange peel, grated<br>¼ tsp. (*1 mL*) almond extract | Add all to yolk mixture and beat well. |
| ¾ cups (*175 mL*) flour<br>1¼ tsp. (*7 mL*) baking powder | Combine, then stir into batter. |
| 3 egg whites | Beat egg whites until stiff. Fold ¼ of the whites into batter to lighten, then fold in the rest. |

Pour batter over fruit mixture and mix well to coat all the fruit and nuts. Line the bottom and sides of one large loaf pan with foil, and butter generously. Spoon batter into prepared pan and cover with buttered aluminum foil.

Bake for 40 minutes. Remove foil from top and continue baking until centre is firm, 15–20 minutes longer.

Cool completely before wrapping with plastic wrap.

*This cake is all nuts and very little batter. It will definitely be a big hit on Christmas day, and the recipe multiplies well for Christmas gift-giving.*

# Aunt B.'s Almond Crescents

Preheat oven to 325°F (*160°C*).

2 cups (*500 mL*) flour
⅛ tsp. (*0.5 mL*) baking powder
½ cup (*125 mL*) sugar

Process together in food processor.

3 egg yolks
1 tsp. (*5 mL*) vanilla

Add and process to mix.

⅘ cup (*200 mL*) cold butter in chunks
1 cup (*250 mL*) almonds, finely ground

Add and process until mixture forms a ball.

Shape into crescents, using ½ Tbsp. (*7 mL*) for each. Place on cookie sheets lined with parchment paper. Bake for 20 minutes until very pale golden (the colour of shortbread). Cool.

Sift icing sugar over crescents. If covered tightly, these can be stored for up to 1 month. Makes about 4 dozen.

*A "melts in your mouth, not in your hand," "bet you can't eat just one" cookie.*

# Pumpkin Praline Pie

1 lightly baked 10″ (*25 cm*) flan crust or deep, 9″ (*23 cm*) pie shell

Preheat oven to 400°F (*200°C*).

## Filling

3 eggs
⅔ cup (*150 mL*) sugar } Beat together until light.

2 cups (*500 mL*) pumpkin purée
½ tsp. (*2 mL*) nutmeg
½ tsp. (*2 mL*) ground ginger
½ tsp. (*2 mL*) allspice
Pinch of salt
1¼ cups (*300 mL*) half and half (light cream)
3 Tbsp. (*45 mL*) brandy } Add rest of ingredients and blend well.

Pour into cooled pie shell. Bake for 15 minutes.

Reduce temperature to 350°F (*180°C*) and bake for an additional 35–40 minutes. Remove from oven and let sit until pie reaches room temperature.

## Topping

¾ cup (*175 mL*) brown sugar
4 Tbsp. (*60 mL*) unsalted butter, melted
2 Tbsp. (*30 mL*) heavy cream
⅔ cup (*150 mL*) pecans, coarsely chopped } Mix all ingredients and spread over pie filling. Place under broiler. Keep turning until topping is evenly brown, being careful not to burn.

| | |
|---|---|
| ½ cup (*125 mL*) heavy cream | Beat until cream stands in soft peaks. |
| 1 tsp. (*5 mL*) vanilla | Add. |

Serve pie warm with whipped cream.

*The crunchy pecan topping is a perfect crown for this new holiday tradition.*

# Pumpkin Chocolate Chip Cake

Preheat oven to 350°F (*180°C*).

| | |
|---|---|
| 4 eggs<br>1 cup (*250 mL*) oil<br>1¾ cups (*425 mL*) sugar | Beat well. |
| 1 14-oz. (*398-mL*) tin pumpkin<br>1 tsp. (*5 mL*) vanilla | Add and mix well. |
| 2 cups (*500 mL*) flour<br>1 cup (*250 mL*) bran<br>2 tsp. (*10 mL*) baking powder<br>1 tsp. (*5 mL*) baking soda<br>1½ tsp. (*7 mL*) cinnamon<br>¼ tsp. (*1 mL*) ground ginger<br>½ tsp. (*2 mL*) allspice<br>¼ tsp. (*1 mL*) cloves<br>Salt and nutmeg to taste | Combine all and add. |
| 2 cups (*500 mL*) chocolate chips (minis are best) | Fold in. |

Pour into well-greased bundt pan. Bake for 50–60 minutes, until toothpick comes out clean. Cover with Mirror Glaze (p. 27) or Chocolate Honey Glaze (p. 119).

*Tasty, hearty lunch-box fare.*

# INDEX